THE ACCIDENTAL
SCREW
Prison Keys & Flying Fleas

John Nixon

Published in 2022 by John Nixon

© Copyright John Nixon

www.johnnixonauthor.co.uk

ISBN: 978-1-913898-39-7

Cover and Book interior Design by Russell Holden

 Pixel Tweaks Publications
SELF PUBLISHING MADE SIMPLE

www.pixeltweakspublications.com

For my wife Philippa who insisted this book be written and throughout was a constant source of inspiration, support and encouragement.

Contents

As always a massive thank you to Russell Holden of Pixel Tweaks who has been part of my writing journey from the very start and who is unfailingly patient with me in spite of my complete ignorance of all things tech.

My thanks also to my lovely sister-in-law Pam over there in Southern Ireland, keeper of Emus and our family photo albums. Couldn't have done it without you.

FOREWORD(S)

I'm sure Haverigg Prison is not entirely unique, but I'd never worked in anywhere quite like it. At the end of WW2, there must have been any number of military sites surplus to requirement. Particularly ex-RAF airfields because of the large acreage they covered, were especially useful for development. So it was on this site, but all they did was take the windswept, sandswept piece of the Cumbrian coast that was the expansion 'drome known as RAF Millom and threw a 15ft fence round it. (You may be somewhat familiar with that old RAF station if you have read any of John Nixon's earlier writings). They just left the old accommodation billets as they were and called it a prison. It was bleak and remote. Prisoners moaned about it, not least how far it was for their visitors to come, but staff also had little choice about their posting. Granted, they built some staff quarters next door and converted some off-site buildings into an officers' club and some bachelor quarters, but it was still at the end of the longest cul-de-sac in England. This some twenty odd years later was what I inherited.

Some focus for my attention when I was sent there as Governor was to give a sense of purpose and added interest for staff and, through them, motivation for prisoners. One way was the setting up of a "project group" which, among other things, produced visual displays of our life as a working prison for such things as Prison Service conferences. One enthusiastic young officer among the group who immediately caught my attention with his bright ideas, skill with a camera and a way with words was John Nixon.

There came a time when it was realised that we were approaching the Prison's 25th anniversary of it's opening- which I quickly saw was also a further 25 years since the opening of the old RAF Millom: 50 years of government service. I didn't feel that occasion should go by without notice. Perhaps we should lay on some activity to involve the local community and to recognise the role of the RAF connection within that community. The general idea was met with mixed enthusiasm and cynicism as to its practicality, but we went ahead. When John Nixon came knocking at my office door, full of enthusiasm, saying he had a long-felt ambition to be a curator of a museum. I saw this as a godsend and send him off with my blessing to drag together the best he could an exhibition of memorabilia. Little did I realise at that stage what I was setting in train: from such a little acorn did a large oak grow! Not just an exhibition for that time, but an ongoing museum for the future.

And so it went on, from dredging a crashed Anson from the estuary to searching the surrounding fells for other debris of wartime. We set up a dedicated workshop which employed a limited number of end- of- life- sentence prisoners who worked with skill and enthusiasm under Officer Nixon's direction.

A highlight for me was the creating of a war memorial to those who had served at RAF Millom and to their mountain rescue teams, and its dedication with full ceremony. The peak of which was a fly-past of RAF Jaguars. My Chaplain had just begun his reading with the line: "…and we shall soar like eagles" when a diamond formation flew over us. That will live in my memory with thanks due to John Nixon for so much hard work and dedication.

In 1997, I retired (now another 25 year's anniversary) and looking back, with the perspective of distant reflection, I can see how much that earlier focus of interest for staff – and, it must be said, prisoners too – made such a difference to the on-going ethos of the prison. Up to me bidding a fond farewell to it all, I realise, with some satisfaction, that the prison had made many strides forward in terms of its ability to make a genuine contribution to the Prison Service. So, thank you John for your enormous contribution to all that.

Bernard Wilson
Former Governor HMP Haverigg

Foreword by Ken Ellis

Pam thought we were barmy. It was March 1994 and we'd arrived at a former mill near Torver, on the western bank of Coniston Water. We met up with John Nixon and his team to remove an unsung piece of Cumberland's aviation heritage and give it new life. Mrs Ellis was even less impressed with the pile of wood, canvas and corroded metal that had been lying forgotten for nearly sixty years. But she was quickly inspired by the zeal and purpose radiating out of John. The remains of this 'Flying Flea', built at Ulverston in 1936, was the first step in John's ambitious scheme to combine rehabilitating offenders with his passion for aviation history.

While we'd previously corresponded on aeronautical matters, it was the 'Flea' that brought John and me together and created a lasting friendship. It was late 1995 when I got to see his 'other side'. HM Prison Haverigg's double gates and its towering wire perimeter conveyed instantly what high security was about. Within was the workshop, inevitably called 'the Hangar'. The Torver 'Flea' had been gloriously completed and the inmates were busy on other tasks. John proudly introduced what he called his 'crew' - Alan, Colin and Dave - and revealed to them that I was covering this unique venture for an article in *FlyPast*. (I was really chuffed with the title I came up with - *Skills Inside* - it took hours!)

I soon realised that whatever had brought these men to Haverigg was irrelevant; here were people keen to turn their lives around. The Governor, John and staff were providing an absorbing and very different way of honing the trio's abilities. Before long we were all talking aeroplanes and techniques and the crew's self-confidence was impressive.

Dominating 'the Hangar' was the fuselage of a 1954 de Havilland Vampire trainer. Already versed in woodworking, Colin had adopted the jet as its structure was mostly moulded ply, but it still looked daunting. John told him how to approach it: "I kept telling myself that this was a lump of wood like any other, and I could work on it."

While restoring a Spitfire elevator, Dave expressed his thoughts on the project: "This isn't something meaningless and repetitive to keep me occupied. I've been asked how I'll tackle it and what I'll need. I've been given a challenge and trusted to deliver on it, that means so much to me."

Alan was building the fuselage of a replica HM.280, developed in the 1940s by the charismatic creator of the 'Flea', Frenchman Henri Mignet. Alan had been poring over the plans to get the 'feel' of the little aeroplane. Clearly motivated, he declared that Mignet's "enthusiasm and vigour gets to you!". Writing this preface many years later, I realised that with those words Alan was also describing the man we've all come to know and love - that's John. You'll enjoy this insightful and engaging book.

Ken Ellis
Aeronautical wordsmith and former editor of *FlyPast* Magazine
People's Republic of Rutland

Introduction

After my seven decades on this planet even a casual glance over my shoulder tells me that my younger years were witness to several local industries and a way of life which has since vanished.

Now happily retired after 32 years serving in Her Majesty's prison service I have bowed to repeated requests for "the prison book" but have decided to start at the beginning because as Mary Poppins said "it's a very good place to start".

I hope that you enjoy the adventures,near death experiences and chaos which characterised my younger years and laugh, as I do now at the farcical way in which I found myself behind bars.

My prison experiences have been varied, challenging, at times upsetting, violent and exhausting but also rewarding latterly as you will see. To all my old colleagues, a big thankyou for your friendship, support and the dark humour which always saw us through difficult times.

John Nixon. 2022.

John Nixon was born in Ulverston, South Lakes, in 1953 and attended High Newton Primary School. Later, on leaving Cartmel Church of England School in 1968, he made his living in varied ways until he joined Her Majesty's Prison Service in 1974. After 32 years service, he is now retired and a self-employed writer. John is also the author of *Wings over Sands* the history of RAF Cark & RAF Grange-over-Sands, and *Warbirds of Walney* the history of RAF Walney Airfield which was shortlisted in the 2014 Lakeland Book of the Year.

CHAPTER ONE

To Begin At The Beginning
Dylan Thomas

Amongst the significant events that occurred in 1953 were: our present Queen ascended the throne; sugar rationing came to an end; Stalin the Russian dictator died age 75; the Royal Yacht Britannia was launched and the brave and hardy Sir Edmund Hillary and Tenzing Norgay became the first men to set foot on the summit of Mount Everest. All that having been said, the most significant event of all that year (for me certainly) was that on the afternoon of the 3rd August, I was born to proud parents, Jack and Margaret Nixon, at Ulverston Cottage hospital, Cumbria!

I've always been a handsome chap but look at that hair - I wish I had even half of it now!

The hospital is now long gone, lost to the Ulverston bypass; a road that contradicts its name by going more or less straight through our town. Now in my 68th year, I live a mere stone's throw from where I was born, literally back where I started.

At this time my father drove lorries for Unsworths in Cartmel but also ran his own business as a timber merchant which he eventually made his full time employment, our family home for the first five years of my life was to be a wooden bungalow on the 'heights' of Cartmel Fell, overlooking the beautiful Winster valley and next door to the Quaker Meeting House of Barrow Wife. During the 17th and 18th centuries the Quakers enjoyed a strong presence on the fell, meeting in each other's houses until 1677, when the meeting house was built. Meetings ceased at Barrow Wife in the 1920's when a new place of worship was built down in Cartmel and the building became a private house. Across from the old meeting house in the Quaker burial ground - still in use today - no grand tombs or statues stand there. Instead each modest stone is a copy of its neighbour, in keeping with the Quaker ethos of equality; an aspiration to be admired and one in rather short supply in these current times.

Dad's old Commer timber wagon

Dad's novel way of keeping me out of mischief

Holly Cottage on Priests Lane in Cartmel, in the shadow of the magnificent Priory, was my father's birth place. Very soon after this his parents, Thomas and Martha, took tenancy at nearby Birkby Hall. They farmed here for a number of years before moving to Greenhurst Farm high up on Bigland Fell between Backbarrow and Field Broughton.

Thomas, my grandfather, bred magnificent Shire horses and won first prizes with them in 1922/23 at the agricultural show at Earl's Court. They were taken down by train and my grandfather camped on the show ground throughout the event.

Grandfather Thomas with one of his award-winning shires.

"SILVER GRILL"
KING'S PREMIUM, THOROUGHBRED AND HUNTER SHOW, AGRICULTURAL HALL,
MARCH 1924, ALSO 1923. SIRE OF INNUMERABLE WINNERS AND CHAMPIONS IN
HUNTER AND LEAPING CLASSES.
GEORGE DICKINSON. CARK MILLS, CARK-IN-CARTMEL.

My Grandfather bred horses along with Mr G.Dickinson of Cark mills He is seen here with Silver Grill a famous award-winning hunter who went on to sire many more champions

My grandmother Martha's maiden name was Pearson. She was the great niece of William Pearson, of Borderside, Cartmel Fell. Born in 1780, William was educated in Crosthwaite and Underbarrow, following which, for a brief period, he was himself teacher at Winster School. It seems that he was not at all settled in that profession. He left to take up employment for a wine merchant in Kendal, before leaving the area to pursue 19 years in banking, down in Manchester. He must have fared well over those years because upon his subsequent return to Cartmel Fell, he purchased Borderside Farm and installed a tenant farmer.

William was somewhat of a rebel. Even before the game laws were amended in 1831, he would openly use his gun to take game wherever he chose, and fished all the becks because he believed that God had made this bounty for everyone. Much of his time at Borderside was spent writing articles on all manner of topics for newspapers and various journals. Simultaneously, he enjoyed a close friendship with William and Dorothy Wordsworth, to whom he sent hay and straw for their horses and fruit from his orchard.

As a confirmed bachelor, it came as a huge surprise to everyone on the Fell that at the age of 61, William decided to marry! His wife Anne was 17 years his junior and the union was a happy one, until his death in 1856. William was buried at Crosthwaite and a bust of him can be found in the church there. He has been an inspiration to my writing and a man I would like to have met.

My mother was born in the village of High Newton; the daughter of Richard and Anne Clark. Always known as Dick to everyone, her father hailed from farming stock near Lowick, though he chose an entirely different path in life. A passionate rum drinker and pipe smoker he fashioned himself into the persona of 'general dealer', becoming very well known in the area. Indeed, some of his 'deals' are the stuff of legend even today.

Anne, my grandmother, had Wilson as her maiden name. She was part of a Romany family which settled in Kendal, during the early 1900's I am told. My gran was fiercely proud of this heritage, but because of it, tracing her family history is all but impossible.

Today's gypsies are enjoying increasing television exposure espousing many weird and contrived traditions and so in many ways, obscuring their true origins. When the Romany people

With Grandpa Dick and his dog Honey, 1958

first made their way into Britain over 500 years ago, they were christened Gypsies because it was thought that they originated from Egypt. The truth is even more amazing, as they are in fact a caste who arrived here from India. Their true language is Sanskrit; the oldest language in the world.

I personally know of no one in the travelling community who is totally fluent in it today, with the language beginning to decline in use from the 1940's onwards and whilst my Gran used many Romany words neither was she fluent in it either.

Three years after my birth my brother Thomas was born and this did not sit well with me at all. I am told that when I was introduced to the new arrival I threw an almighty tantrum and told my parents to take him back and get me a sister. I am fortunate that I have several 'snapshot' memories of our five years on the fell: my pet hen, drawing water from a nearby stream when our pipes froze during our last winter there, but my fondest and most vivid memory is of being in my pushchair on the road to High Newton reservoir and my Mum picking up a fluffy curlew chick and allowing me to cuddle it.

In 1958 we left the fell and went to live in the village of High Newton. My parents had purchased Queens Arms cottage, a partially converted coaching inn. It was one of three which had existed in the village to serve travellers during the coaching years. Aside from the Queens Arms there had been the Horse and Farrier and the Crown Hotel. The Horse and Farrier, like the Queens Arms, is now a house but the Crown still does business today and its food and beers are to be recommended.

Upon arriving at our new home, work to modernise it began almost straight away. To facilitate the process we all moved into the property's huge attic, which was a big adventure. Another great adventure at this time, though not as welcome, was my beginning primary school. I can remember registering my disgust that I had to go to school, but brother Thomas did not. In actuality I began what was to be six wonderful years of varied and engaging education.

My school days begin

High Newton School, opened in 1875 and closed in 1970. Now a village hall

The experience I enjoyed at High Newton Primary School was entirely due to the kindness and wisdom of our teacher. Mrs Baines opened my eyes to the wider world, its peoples, flowers and fauna, igniting in me a thirst for literature and a burning desire to travel. I have happy memories of nature walks, our annual nativity play and being taken bird watching after school by Mrs Baines and her husband. It is a tragedy that over the years we have lost so many of our little village schools and the gentle introduction they provided to education.

The 1950's were a very different time. Looking at them from a multicultural point of view, I can clearly recall when I saw my first person of mixed race. The chap was plastering one of our rooms in the cottage and I blurted out to my mother, "That man is black!" He picked up a piece of wet plaster and scored a perfect hit on the back of my head with it as I took flight. I had already seen the look on his face.

As in Dylan Thomas's fishing village of Llaregubb, the 'characters' in our village were several and varied. At the top of the village lived a woman called Dorothy Jones, who suffered mental health issues. If she got wind that we kids were near her house, she'd erupt from her door shouting all sorts of random chastisements at us, causing us to flee to the safety of home.

A mixed class of ten with Mrs Baines. Looking left to right along the back row are:
Penny Hemmingway, myself, Joyce Barker and Paul Stoker.
On the front row left to right are: Sydney Ormord, Jonathan Stoker, my brother
Thomas, Edward Rawesthorn, Geoffrey Barker & Nicola Walker

Further along the village was my father's brother, Uncle Jim. A very quiet chap, Jim loved anything mechanical and was always taking stuff to bits. His silence, focus and general behaviour suggest to me now that he was somewhere on the Asperger's spectrum, but in village parlance he was just a 'cob lad' (strange). Following the death of his wife, he would work on mechanical items in his front room, resulting in oil stains on his settee. One day my horrified father found him trying to swab them off with a can of petrol and a rag ... in front of a roaring open fire! A 'cob lad' indeed.

As Joseph in the school
nativity play

Also resident in our village and largely looked upon with disapproval was a chap called Tom Shaw, a portly widower and regular customer of the Crown Hotel. It seems that he was incapacitated in some way as he received benefits. There were those who said that he was once a council worker, but his pursuit of any gainful employment

With Mum and dad's huge Hudson Terraplane car. An American vehicle that was so roomy we could all camp in it.

was so far back in the mists of time, that no one would swear to it. Towards the end of his life he would occasionally help behind the bar in the Crown, all the while sweating profusely; a bead of sweat on his scarlet nose often dripping into the pint he was pulling.

Then there was David Reid, from Low Newton, who went off into Lancashire to work for a few weeks with an Irish road gang. He came home with a thick Irish brogue - which he affected for the rest of the time I knew him - earning him the nickname 'Irish Davey'. We made our own entertainment back then.

A sort of uncle on my mother's side lived next door to us: Uncle Bill. Now Bill had that thing that fascinates young lads the most: a shed full of 'stuff'. He was however a man of little patience, with a spiteful sense of humour and would play tricks on me. I now see with the passage of time that these were quite cruel. I clearly remember going into his shed one morning to see what was happening and accidently cracked the corner of an old piece of glass that he had propped against his bench. This earned me a back handed blow to the side of the head that knocked me clean out of the door and on to the garden path. Many of that generation were free and easy with their hands in those days. My overall memories of the old bugger are of him slouched in his chair by his open coal fire, smoking a pipe and spitting phlegm into the grate, as though determined to extinguish the flames.

My Mum was a keen horsewoman and tried to encourage an interest in me by buying this Shetland pony called Juju. But it was not to be. The Shetland is the Jack-Russell of the equine world and after being bitten by by new pal and thrown off twice he was sold to become the mount of some other unsuspecting child.I had learned all I need to know about horses - one end of them bites - and the other end of them shites!

My dad's mum, our Grannie Nixon, was a quiet soul who seemed to just let all things go over her head. She lived in the village along with my two maiden aunts, Eleanor and Mary. The two sisters were polar opposites. Aunt Mary was the kindest woman you could imagine, always with time for us kids and a lovely sense of fun. She died after a long and cruel illness when I was 12 years old and I miss her to this day. Aunt Eleanor, in contrast, was a somewhat spiteful woman, prone to throwing herself into a foul mood or a full blown rage at the slightest perceived provocation. The following incident has made me smile over the years, but today we would call it a bizarre form of child abuse:

My Dad and my Mum had booked a coach trip to Blackpool for the day and myself and brother Thomas were to be left at our Grannie Nixon's for the day. Mum had given both of us pocket money. I decided to head straight away to our village shop and spend it on sweets. I came back to gran's and sat eating my toffees whilst reading a comic, when dear Aunt Eleanor returned home from work. After a few moments of watching me munching happily on my treats, my dear old aunt threw a full blown tantrum, calling me a greedy pig and a glutton! Knowing full well that she was a bit doolally I began laughing and this precipitated a full blown meltdown. She stormed off into their pantry and brought back her treat tin full of chocolate and other sundry goodies. She threw the loaded tin into my lap and shouted to my bemused gran, "Right, let's see how much the greedy little swine can eat. Go on eat it!" she shrieked, all the while becoming redder in the face. So I began: there was a Mars bar; a Blue Ribbon biscuit; a couple of small bars of chocolate - all quite delicious - and several other items I cannot recall. About halfway through the tin however, I began to feel a little queasy and told my dear old aunt that I did not wish to continue. But, by now she was apoplectic, incandescent and out of control, insisting that I was not leaving the house until I had finished the lot. My encroaching nausea and previous amusement turned now to pure spite and so I ploughed on, though my rate of consumption had slowed somewhat. The last item I managed to force down was a Fry's Fruit Chocolate Cream and I have never been able to face one since. I felt as sick as the proverbial dog, but I won! I could tell that my gran was impressed, but my aunt was seething; she snatched the empty tin from me and stormed off. My satisfaction at beating her almost outweighed the awful stomach cramps I experienced as I spent the next ten minutes projectile vomiting onto her compost heap. Victory can be costly and hard won.

Within our small community there were few people who had travelled extensively, if at all, save for those who had served overseas during the war. As such, the general outlook of the village was somewhat parochial. When I was around eight years old a young man became a family friend. Bill Teasdale was 14 years my senior and I came to regard him as an older brother figure. Bill came from a Quaker family and had been schooled by Quakers over in Yorkshire, which made him somewhat philosophical in nature and even a young boy like myself knew that he was different. Bill was a Cartmel lad, but village life was never going to be enough for him. Acting on an impulse he sailed off to Italy and had many adventures there, before returning home, all the more restless and eager to see more of the world.

It was around this time that my mother and father were seriously considering emigrating to Australia as 'Ten Pound Poms'. In the end, and after much deliberation, my father decided against the move. Bill however, decided that a better life was to be had on the other side of the world and in 1961 sailed off to a new life in West Australia, aboard the Oriana. Bill settled in Perth where he married Maureen - who was also from Cartmel and built a good life for themselves and their two children, Angie and Stuart. In retirement I have spent a good deal of time over in Perth with them and enjoyed some fantastic road trips with Bill; two old guys reminiscing about old times, barrelling down those endless dusty bush roads and misbehaving at every opportunity. With his 'can do' approach to life, Bill still fills that 'older brother' place in my life.

He would be most annoyed if I failed to point out also that he has cultivated what is possibly the finest beard in West Australia!

Mum went on to breed Shetlands in later life, and as you can see, she was very hands on with them.

Bushman Bill Teasdale, Kalbari National Park WA.

High Newton has changed a great deal over my lifetime. Not only has the village school been lost, but when I was a boy the village could boast a resident District Nurse, a Post Office/General Store and a well stocked grocery shop; all long gone now. All in all, my primary school years were happy ones. I recall snowy winters and gloriously warm summers wandering the surrounding fells, building dens and having great adventures. My Dad's work in the woods meant that my mum, brother Thomas and I would often go off there with him on weekends. Mum would cook over an open fire for us and we would spend the day adventuring and looking for bird nests. We both loved it, but for my brother it became a vocation and Thomas followed Dad into the wood business after moving to Southern Ireland, where he now lives.

Like most kids of the time, Thomas and I fell prey to various childhood illnesses: mumps (face like a pumpkin); impetigo (great

Mr and Mrs Harrison, who farmed in our village kept a pet deer which us kids would feed buns to. Here are myself, Geoffrey and Joyce Barker doing just that in Mrs Harrison's kitchen.

for scab picking) and chicken pox (pick those spots and you get a face like a lunar landscape for life).but I did not contract measles until I was 17 years old, having caught them due to rather close contact with a very pretty girl. It made me quite ill, but then there is a price to be paid for everything.

From the moment I began to read, and with the encouragement of my teacher, reading became almost an obsession. I would read anything I could get my hands on. I read the usual children's books such as Rupert Bear, before moving on to various classics: some Dickens, Treasure Island, Swiss Family Robinson, The Coral Island, King Solomon's Mines and any other adventure stories I could find. I'd read until the early hours under my blankets with a torch. Towards the end of Primary School, my reading became increasingly eclectic, encompassing just about anything that sparked my interest.

 And so it was that when I came of age, I was expected to breeze through my 11 plus exam and toddle off to Grammar School. However, this was not to be. After staring blankly at the somewhat confusing exam paper for a while and failing to give it my full attention, I realised that it was not some fine Grammar School for the gifted that awaited me, but instead Cartmel Priory Church of England Secondary School was to be my lot.

My family made it abundantly clear that they had expected much better from me and of course my dear Aunt Eleanor was furious. Conversely, my Aunt Mary took me to one side, gave me half a crown and told me not to worry about it. In truth I was not worried in the least. I had enjoyed Primary School under Mrs Baines and simply expected more of the same. I was keen to broaden my knowledge of Geology, History and Geography, my three main interests at the time and so after a gentle and happy cradling throughout my early school years,I felt set fair for what was to come.

CHAPTER TWO

When I Think of all The Crap I Learned in High School, It's a Wonder I Can Think at all

Paul Simon

My summer holidays flew by and the great day arrived at last! Children from around our area were transported to school by minibus. Driven by a chap called John Battersby, naturally it was known as "Bats Bus". As I climbed aboard it for my first day at secondary school I was certainly excited, but also very nervous. Arriving at Cartmel School that morning I recall no welcome or induction process. My vivid memory is one of standing in what seemed to be a huge yard, which was thronged with kids who were all strangers to me and who considered us 'first years' to be no better than pond life.

Somewhat timidly, I set about exploring my new surroundings. I wandered quite innocently around a corner to the school's bicycle sheds where I came across a group of older boys smoking cigarettes. This was to be the first (but not the last) time in my life that I would be instructed to "Fuck off!" The 'F word' was completely new to me but I understood the "off" bit well enough and beat a hasty retreat.

Secondary school days

In my later years in the Prison Service the exclamation of "Fuck off" served almost as a conversation opener between prisoners and their keepers.

The young smoker who had dismissed me in this fashion was to become my nemesis and bully me unmercifully during my time at Cartmel. His name was Mike and I was by no means his only victim. Mike had lips that would have made Mick Jagger appear lacking in that department and behind his back those he persecuted called him "Rubber Lips". One of the most glorious scenes I ever witnessed was the day that Mike got into a confrontation with another (larger) bully. A heated argument went on for several minutes before the conflict was brought to an abrupt end by the larger bully, who, having become bored with the confrontation, simply kicked Mike in the balls…hard! My heart sang as Mike made a strangled sound and doubled over looking as though he was closely examining his shoes. Realising this spectacle had been seen by us all, our amusement and satisfaction were short lived as he redoubled his bullying over the following weeks, in order to regain some respect once again from his victims.

Each school day began with a religious assembly in the school gymnasium where we would all sing hymns. This was presided over by a teacher who we nicknamed "Goat". He would march through our ranks, all the while singing loudly and badly himself, seeking out anyone purposely singing the wrong words or misbehaving in some way. He could generally catch two or three at each assembly. After a cuff around the head, you would be led by a pinched ear to line up for caning outside the Headmaster's office. This took the form of six blows across the back of your legs with a hazel stick and it stung like hell.

It would serve no purpose to dwell overlong upon my Secondary School years, suffice to say that I loathed them. I realise now that I was passing through a 'one size fits all' education system, which inspired me not one bit. With some exceptions I did not respect my teachers at all, but instead feared them and from this fear sprang an intense dislike and anger. As I have grown older I have come to understand them to some degree. Several of them would have served their country during the Second World War and if not serving, they had lived through that dreadful time. It has brought me to realise that the couple of teachers I liked and did respect, were more patient and understanding because they were much younger than the rest of the staff; staff that it is fair to say did not spare the rod and in some cases were downright mean.

A good example of this springs to mind: During lunch in the school dining hall one day, I threw a piece of boiled potato at someone and thought I had got away with it. The teacher on dining hall duty that day was our woodwork teacher, a dour, ill tempered individual we had nicknamed "Snudge". Woodwork was to be our first lesson after lunch and upon our arrival in the classroom I was ordered to follow him into the wood storeroom. Once there and with no preamble at all, I was bent over a sawhorse and beaten across the back of my legs with a length of dowling until I felt physically sick. Some days later my mother saw the injuries and asked how I had come by them. I told her, but do not recall her reaction; these were different times. I do believe that more discipline is required in schools today, but cannot mourn the passing of corporal punishment, having myself been at the mercy of those who were a bit too ready with their hands and sticks.

The highlight of my secondary school years was a walking and geology field trip into the surrounding Lake District. Our small group stayed in a Youth Hostel at Cockley Beck, which closed some years ago. We spent a good part of our stay walking on the surrounding fells and I loved it. From that time onwards my love of the fells was firmly established; I have run and walked them all my life. The trip was staffed by our younger teachers, who I am sure enjoyed the time as much as we all did, laughing and joking with us and generally exerting just enough discipline to keep us all in order.

Now the Whitewater Hotel, the Blue Mill once dominated the skyline with its tall chimney which was removed following its closure

My family could not be described as 'well off' by any means, but their work ethic was very strong. My mother and father both worked and were unfailing providers; we never saw a hungry day. During the time I was at secondary school my mother did various jobs, including cleaning the village school. Meanwhile, dad worked at the Backbarrow Blue Mills and for a time on the Backbarrow bypass, having left the timber business due to lack of demand. When the bypass was completed he alternated between working at the Backbarrow IronWorks in winter and the Lake Windermere Steamers in summer. When the IronWorks closed down in 1967, rather than be unemployed, my father spent the next two winters at sea on an Icelandic trawler operating out of Fleetwood. This would without

Dad in his role as greaser in the engine room of a Boston trawler out of Fleetwood.

17

doubt have been a harsh and dangerous work environment, but incredibly dad seems to have enjoyed the experience. In his later years he looked back fondly on his time at sea, as somewhat of an adventure. In the fullness of time my dad became part of the permanent staff at Lakeside, sailing the summer months and carrying out maintenance on the vessels in winter. In 1970 he became a captain, skippering the MV Swift and the MV Tern, before taking exclusive captainship of the MV Swan in 1974.

It seems unbelievable in this day and age of health and safety, but whilst dad was working at the Backbarrow Iron Works, he would often take me to work with him, frequently for a night shift. My school pal, Mike Stretch, lived very close to the Works and we would meet up there. We would brew tea for the workmen and heat their food for them, on the gang hut coke stoves. It was all a great experience for two young lads.

At the Works there were four huge bunkers, right next to the railway line and the train pulled trucks alongside which tipped directly into them. There was one bunker each for iron ore, coke, limestone and best of all one for scrap metal of various sorts. The scrap heap was huge and Mike and I would clamber all over it looking for items we could swap at school. Magnets especially were a very valuable swapping item. Neither Mike nor I could believe our good fortune when the Royal Artillery range, up the coast at

Backbarrow Iron Works, early 1960s.
Courtesy Richard Sanderson

Raking slag from the ladle's surface before casting. *Courtesy Richard Sanderson*

Eskmeals, began sending their scrap to Backbarrow. In it were all sorts of goodies: shell cases, empty mortar cases complete with fins and all kinds and sizes of inert shell heads. We became kings of the school swap overnight.

The smelting and casting process was fascinating and because we were so young, Mike and I must be the only two people alive today who could share vivid memories of it. To release the molten metal from the furnace, a huge crowbar was used to break the clay plug. The plug was used after each casting to reseal what was known as the 'eye'. Mike and I were often allowed to have a go at breaking the plug, but nine times out of ten we could not do it, much to the amusement of the casting gang. The molten metal would flow into a huge ladle which was moved around the casting shed by the cab operator on an overhead electric crane. Using a wheel located on the side of the ladle, the molten ore was poured into rows of sand moulds. The resulting bars were known as 'pigs' or 'pig iron'. This was because the rows of bars all branched from a central channel, resembling suckling piglets.

Despite the nature of the industry there seemed to be few accidents or injuries, certainly during dad's time there. However,

Mike Stretch and I were witness to a catastrophic event during a winter's night casting that had the potential to have ended very differently. The ladle had been filled and had just been moved. It was approaching the casting point when the ladle operator lost control of the tipping wheel. How this happened has never been clear to me, but it was obvious that what was about to happen was deadly serious. A shout went up, "Run! The bugger's going to go!" Seeing the scene below him, the crane operator began moving the gradually tipping ladle down to the end of the casting shed away from everyone. As he reached the end of the shed it finally emptied itself, straight into an area of standing water. It is impossible to describe the display of pyrotechnics that ensued; globules of semi molten metal flew through the air like meteorites and the overhead crane caught fire. As the crane driver abandoned his cab, Mike and I stood transfixed throughout the disaster. It is amazing to me now that no one got so much as a scratch. Imagine a 12 year old boy being allowed into an environment like that today. It would most definitely result in a visit from social services.

What remains of the ironworks today is being preserved and restored in a project driven by Richard Sanderson (bottom right)

20

My dad was a great one for making 'things' and improvising. However, he was nothing short of a liability where electricity was involved. I clearly remember arriving home from school one day to find my mother fuming, the house fuses blown and a potato knife welded into the kitchen light socket. Dad never passed up on any item that might be of future use and had acquired from somewhere a carborundum wheel with the hope of fixing it to an electric motor for his outhouse workshop, due to the absence of such a motor the hunt was on. Like Mike and myself Dad began combing the ironwork's scrapheap for just such an item and was overjoyed when he found one - a substantial sized machine that would surely be fit for such a project. My dad had a robust workbench made from railway sleepers. My brother and I watched one morning as he bolted this large motor to it and set about trying to fathom a way of fixing the grinding wheel onto its shaft. This proved problematic as the hole in the wheel was a good deal bigger than the diameter of the shaft. Not to be beaten, my dad made a sleeve from a piece of metal pipe and then drove in a series of brass wedges to hold it in place…what could go wrong? Total genius! Next were the electrics. Dad had a unique way of connecting workshop devices. He would shove two bare wires into a wall socket and jam them in with matchsticks - no need to fuss around with a plug at all.

So having spun said wheel a couple of times to establish that it was running true, Dad gave the command "Stand back" and plugged in his new creation. This abandoned motor, given the kiss of life once more, began turning with an enthusiastic hum, which swiftly rose to a whine and then became a scream. Smoke and sparks began to issue forth at an alarming rate. It was clear that this out of control device was built to drive something much more substantial than a mere grinding wheel. It continued to accelerate with Dad hopping left and right, but lacking the raw nerve to reach over it and pull out the wires. Now, seeing the wheel begin to wobble on the motor's shaft, Dad issued his next command "Run!"…and we did! Just as the wheel left the motor, skidded across the bench and up the wall breaking into several pieces.

The motor, now unfettered in any way, simply blew up and with it once again, so did our house fuse box. This prompted a visit from my irate mum, who informed Dad in a most colourful way, that his days of "buggering about with electricity were at an end. I recall many adventures with Dad after that, but thankfully none involving electricity.

During my last summer holidays from secondary school Mum was working in the café on Lakeside Pier and Dad was crewing on the MV Swift. This meant that brother Thomas and I would go along with them and were free to entertain ourselves in any way we chose. To me this was fishing and adventuring; the sun seemed to shine every day. I recall these days as being a time of total freedom and a precious memory. My brother feels differently however. He regards himself as having been a 'latchkey kid'. Me...? I thought I was Tom Sawyer.

The Lakeside and station of my youth. Bottom left MV Swan in original configuration. Top right the M Swift docking at Lakeside for the final time in 1981. *Photos courtesy of Rob Beale*

Brother Thomas and I enjoyed a somewhat combative relationship as we grew up; nothing more than the usual sibling rivalry and not least of all due to the fact that we were so unalike, as siblings often are. I spent all my teens rudderless whilst he, always one for hard manual work, knew what he wanted from life and has made a good one for himself, his wife Pamela and their six children over in Southern Ireland.

The modified lines of the Swan today

CHAPTER THREE

If You Don't Know Where You're Going
Any Road Will Take You There
George Harrison

As my final school report suggests, I was very interested in that which I found interesting and anything else, more or less, went over my head. Mathematics was, and remains, a mystery to me. To suggest that a letter can be a number seems preposterous and contrary to common sense. Having left school (I thought of it more as escaping), I daydreamed through the summer months without a care and gave little thought as to what my working life was to entail. With no O'Levels or obvious skills neither I, nor anyone else, had a clue as to what the hell I was going to do with regard to securing gainful employment.

Still doggedly suspecting that I was hiding my light under a bushel, my parents decided that further education was the answer and would help me buckle down at last, perhaps finally able to fulfil my academic potential. I simply went along with the idea, it seemed a soft option as manual labour appealed to me not one little bit. The institution chosen to affect this miracle was the Lancaster and Morecambe College of Further Education. I was enrolled to study chemistry, physics, biology, statistics and English literature at O'Level, beginning in the autumn of 1968.

At once I realised that this was education at a completely different level and I enjoyed the classroom environment, without the constrictions (and corporal punishment) I had bitterly resented at Cartmel School. It is unfortunate in the extreme that around this time however, I began to develop three entirely new interests: rock music, motorcycles and girls. The avid pursuit of these interests began to clash with my studies somewhat. Many half day absences from college resulted and were idled away in Lancaster's coffee houses, the Ramblers Café in Morecambe, Ed's Snooker Hall and the odd bar when funds allowed. Obviously, this sort of errant behaviour was only going to produce one outcome. Sure enough, one fine spring morning I was summoned to the college principal's office. I was tactfully informed that it would be in everyone's best interests if I were to abandon any academic aspirations I might still harbour and instead seek employment of some description. When I told the sad news to my parents my mum broke down in tears, but Dad was more forthright, telling me that I had let the family down and that I should get a job immediately. I felt deeply ashamed at having cost them a good deal of money in offering me the opportunity to gain qualifications and a chance at a decent career.

Following this debacle I straight away went to work on the Lake Windermere Steamers and in doing so was able to save enough money to buy my first motorcycle. I rode this machine with such competence and panache that I may as well have bought a revolver instead and spent my time playing Russian roulette with it! I had many spills, but my most spectacular accident occurred when I took a right turn in front of an articulated lorry at Newby Bridge. I remember executing this manoeuvre and then nothing more until I found myself staring up at the wagon's front axle. A trip to hospital, several stitches, a visit from the police and two weeks later I was back at work once again, riding my newly repaired steed once more, once again with the aforementioned competence and panache.

During 1969 my parents were building a bungalow for us across the village on what had been Dad's wood yard. Dad was employing a builder called George Jackson, a highly skilled bloke who always had a good story to tell and could be relied upon to offer profound and wise advice.

The following culminates in his most memorable offering:

I had spent the previous evening underage drinking in Ulverston. Quite merry from it, I had filled my time waiting for my bus home by kissing and cuddling a pretty girl in a doorway by the bus station. This had not gone unseen and had been witnessed by two elderly and righteous folk from our village who were returning from bingo. Outraged by this shameful spectacle they felt it was their moral duty to inform my mother, who became similarly outraged with dire consequences for me. I was helping George at the bungalow site when my mother stormed onto the scene. In a colourful manner she straight away began admonishing me for bringing shame on our family. She followed this with a lecture about sex before marriage being a sin. I thought that George might have tried to mediate in some way, but he seemed to be taking my mum's side, looking at me sadly and shaking his head. Having vented her ire and recieving my assurance that I understood, so that there would be no repeat of this scandalous behaviour, she finally left. Putting down his trowel George placed a finger on my chest and with each word accompanied by a prod, said sternly, "Remember: sex – before – marriage – is – a – sin!" Then lighting a cigarette and picking up his trowel he added "And sex after marriage is a bloody miracle!" then roared with laughter.

As the summer of 1969 drew to a close and the Windermere Steamers were laid up for winter maintenance once again, I began to look for employment elsewhere. In those days there could be up to three pages of job vacancies in our local paper. Among them I found a vacancy for an apprentice welder/sheet metal worker at a firm in Ulverston called Acrastyle.

The factory was situated right next to the canal there and manufactured huge immersion tanks and electrical cabinets for various companies, including the Ford Motor plant at Dagenham in Essex. I began work there in mid October in the metal fabrication shop and whilst the work was dirty and at times hard, I found it interesting. It seems incredible now, but my wage there was £4-10 a week (four pounds and ten shillings), which today would just about buy one pint of beer or six bags of crisps.

Acrastyle was a non union firm and as such they moved an employee around as they saw fit. In my case, I soon found myself working in the paint spraying department. The firm's customers demanded a very high gloss finish on the electrical cabinets. This was achieved by spraying them firstly with a low bake enamel paint, which was then heat dried. Following this, I and another young workmate, would have to sand down the finish using progressively finer wet and dry paper, before burnishing it back to a mirror finish. It was an arduous and boring task which took a long time, leaving us with very little skin on our fingertips. We hated it. The man who ran the spray shop was a perfectionist and a bully. At the end of our labours we would show him what appeared to us to be a perfect finish, only to see him shake his head, take out his car keys and scoring a zig zag scratch across the panel he would announce, "Useless! Rub it down, we'll do it again." He would simply wander off whistling, but for us it was soul destroying. However, we became so good at this task that we got 80% of our efforts past him as time went on.

The winter of 1969-70 was a severe one. The canal froze to such an extent that we would play football on it during our lunch break. It was also a cold journey from High Newton to Ulverston by motorbike. I would pull in at Greenodd Railway Station - which was on the old Lakeside Line - to smoke a fag and warm my hands on the bike's exhaust, before undertaking the last five miles to work.

By the spring of 1970 and still stuck in the spray shop that I was heartily sick of, my thoughts turned to escape. I tendered a week's notice in early April, before going to work once more on Lake Windermere. During my final day in the spray shop I was working hard on a huge electrical panel, which I was told had to be finished before I would be allowed to leave. At the end of the working day I had almost completed the job and I asked Fred, the workshop manager, if I could clock off. His reply was "No. You stay here till it's finished and I'm happy with it, you idle little shit!" About an hour later I called him over to inspect the completed article and it was such a good job I knew that he would have to pass it.

The lovely Greenodd Station. Now replaced with a dual carriageway

He did, dismissing me with "Ok, you can bugger off home now." Fred then wandered off out of the paint shop with his customary whistling. Seizing my opportunity I took out my motorbike key and scratched "GOODBYE" deep into the immaculate finish on the panel, before hightailing it home, all the way laughing fit to burst.

There are often periods in our lives that upon reflection seem to go on forever. For me they were the summers of 1969 and 1970, working on the Windermere Steamers. I was just about as happy and carefree as I've ever been in my life, but as usual with the 1970 sailing season drawing to a close once more, I was left seeking employment for the coming winter months. A plumbing and heating firm based in our village was looking for someone for general fetching and carrying; I got the job. The wages were decent, but the owner suffered badly from 'little man syndrome' and I struggled to like him at all. Being the dogsbody I got just about every unpleasant job there was and I had nothing at all in common with the men I was working with. After several unhappy months, I was on the verge of handing in a week's notice when the question of whether to or not to do so resolved itself.

One of the tasks I was often given was putting the fittings into the central heating oil tanks and painting them. These were usually situated in the homeowner's or property's garden area. On this occasion I was working at a house owned by one of my old school teachers. I had fitted out the tank, painted it and was waiting for a tanker to arrive to fill it. Having duly arrived the tanker driver and I wasted no time in coupling up to the tank, adjourning to the garden shed for a brew and chinwag. A short while later, my driver pal went out to check on progress and had only been gone a few seconds when he let out an almighty roar, "Oh shit! Oh shite! No, no. Somebody hasn't put the drain plug in. It's all over the bloody garden!" And indeed it was. Despite my best and frantic efforts it proved impossible to stem the flow of heating oil, even though the tank had not been filling for long. Even to my untrained eye, it seemed highly unlikely that anything would thrive in the surrounding vegetable patch anytime soon, oh dear.

What transpired next is open to conjecture. I gave my boss my resignation just as he told me I was fired. Each of us stuck to our opinion as to whether I was jumping or being pushed. A heated and somewhat one sided discussion then took place, at the end of which - as in those school days of yore - I was told to fuck off, which I did.

Once more unemployed, I was content in the knowledge that the Windermere boats would soon be hiring again and for the time being at least I would be spared the spectre of permanent employment. My transition from pipe bender, tank painter, trench digger and general dogsbody to another blissful season as a Windermere deckhand was not to be seamless. I took a stopgap job as a café waiter in Grange-over-Sands (think Fawlty Towers character Manuel), until the summer sailing season started.

It was whilst working in Grange that I rekindled what had been a brief college relationship, with an attractive blonde girl called Fay. Unlike me, Fay had buckled down to her studies at Lancaster and was now working at a hair salon in Grange.

As that summer passed, Fay and I fell in love and began to think that we might have a future together.

Love is a form of madness and brings about a state of mind which convinces those thus afflicted that it will conquer all; that green pastures and blue skies await all those who fall prey to it. Love, however, requires commitment (not my strong suit) and a serious vision for the future if matrimony is to be in the offing. It is also important that the couple in question have a reasonable amount of capital and that the husband has a steady job. At this point I had neither.

CHAPTER FOUR

It Takes a Lot to Laugh,
It Takes a Train to Cry
Bob Dylan

As the Windermere season came to an end and the boats were moored for winter, there was a new urgency to my job seeking. A vacancy appeared in our newspaper for a job on British Rail, working in the freight yard in Ulverston. I was taken on straight away as they were desperate to fill the post but it meant that I had to attend a medical board retrospectively in the coming weeks.

It is difficult to imagine today how busy the sidings were then; they served both Glaxo and local industries. My job involved logging in and out chemical tanks, boxcars and flat wagons known as conflats. I also used to work with a gang manually unloading cargo from the boxcars. A common load was bags of something called Limbux. I have no idea what it was, but it was like lime or cement and I think meant for the building industry. I loved the job from the very start and worked with a great crew. They treated me as an equal, including me in after work beers in the Station Hotel across the road from the freight yard. There was always some good natured leg pulling and banter. The part of the job I enjoyed the most was delivering the large full oil and chemical tanks to the Glaxo complex in south Ulverston and bringing the empties back to the station sidings. This would involve travelling down the mainline to Plumpton Junction where at a signal box (now removed) one line spur left east for the track which terminated at Lakeside Station via Greenodd. A second line spur doubled back from the mainline and ran into Glaxo.

31

By this time the Lakeside line was closed and the track was being taken up. However, the line into Glaxo remained active until the 1990's, with the track finally being removed in 1994. With myself riding either in the driver's cab with him or in a guard's van at the rear, the journey involved crossing the Ulverston Canal. The canal was designed by architect John Rennie and was opened to traffic from the Leven estuary in 1796. It has the distinction of being the shortest, broadest and deepest in Britain.

Our crossing of the canal was made via what had originally been an electrically operated rolling bridge. This ingenious structure was designed by engineer Frank Stileman in 1893. It facilitated a locomotive crossing to what was then Ulverston Iron Works, whilst allowing the passage of waterborne traffic. Powered by a large generator which was housed in a tall building nearby, the centre section of the bridge would retract on its large steel wheels into a huge bay on the west bank of the canal. Following the closure of the canal, the bridge was fixed in its present position and the receiving bay filled in. It is noteworthy that the Stileman rolling bridge is the only one of its kind in existence and a Grade two listed structure.

This part of the structure slid into a bay to the right of the photograph.

Here's how she rolled

End of the line

A working model of the bridge

After working at the freight yard for several weeks I was finally sent off to Manchester for my medical. Thinking it a mere formality, the results of my examination would however, once again see me unemployed. I was found to be colour blind and as my duties at the yard could be varied and colour signals were crucial to the rail network, I was informed that sadly they would have to let me go, but with a glowing reference for any other job I might apply for. Now that was a first! I was genuinely upset and disappointed to lose the job and trudged off home to inform everyone that once again I was considered an employment liability. Although this time, it was through no fault of my own.

Following this unforeseen loss of income, I was once again on the lookout for a job. Any job. But within a week I had managed to find employment at Newby Bridge Motors. For a while I did a little paint spraying, mended punctures, pumped a lot of fuel and almost blinded myself.

The garage regularly had batteries brought in for charging and I usually got the job. This involved removing the caps from the cells before coupling the thing up to a charger. When charging was deemed to be nearing completion, the acid in the battery could be seen to bubble merrily and produce (I was to learn the hard way) hydrogen gas. The device used to ascertain whether or not a full charge had been achieved, consisted of two metal rods. One rod was to be placed on each battery terminal and a gauge between them gave a voltage reading. On the morning in question I had disconnected a large battery from the charger. Without replacing the cell caps, I applied the device to the battery terminals which caused a blue flash igniting the gas in the cells, explosively spraying acid into my face. I ran outside and from memory located the tyre bath full of filthy water and plunged my head and shoulders into it. This without doubt saved my eyes and skin from certain damage, but left me to return to my labours in a less than fragrant condition.

Whilst I was working at the garage, we were frequently overflown at low level by the huge Avro Vulcan nuclear strike bombers, which were carrying out exercises over the Lake District mountains. This was really exciting for me as I had developed a keen interest in aircraft, as far back as my primary school time. With my Dad, we made regular visits to deliver wood to a family who actually lived in the old control tower, on the disused WWII airfield at Cark, in Cartmel. One slightly frosty morning with low lying fog, I heard the unmistakable howl as a Vulcan approached the garage. The plane came in at an incredibly low altitude, heading straight for and then climbing up the flank of Gummers How fell with a noise like thunder; dark exhaust trails pouring from its huge engines. So low was its pass that around ten minutes later and for a while afterwards, the smell of aviation fuel lingered in the low lying mist.

Garage work was not for me and it's fair to say that the couple who owned the business were less than broken-hearted when I announced that I was leaving for yet another season on the Windermere boats. I have many memories from my days working on the lake and all are happy ones but two recollections from my 1973 season remain vivid.

By this time my Dad had been promoted to skipper and I often worked alongside him. On this particular occasion we were crewing the MV Tern and making our way from Bowness to Ambleside when we saw a tall pillar of smoke rising from the lake, among a large gathering of yachts. As we drew closer, we could see that the beautiful vintage launch the Royal Windermere Yacht Club were using as a judges' grandstand had somehow caught fire and was well on its way to being completely destroyed. It was clear to us that all those on board the launch had been taken off, so without further ado we came alongside and Dad ordered the hoses out, much to the excitement and delight of our passengers. Sadly, I don't think that the launch was deemed salvageable and we never did find out what had started the fire. We received a letter of thanks from the yacht club for extinguishing the blaze and our actions were subsequently immortalised in the Westmorland Gazette.

Some weeks later, on a fine sunny day, not far from where this last incident took place we were again on the MV Tern. My crewmate, Brian Wilkinson, spotted two lads in a rowing boat, waving frantically and pointing to a figure some distance from them in the water. Clearly help was required, so we drew closer to investigate. We could see that the figure in the water was in fact a female who was clutching an oar for buoyancy and requesting, in a very Australian accent, to be removed from "the bloody lake", or words to that effect. With some careful manoeuvring from us and some effort from the young woman, we managed to get her alongside, but there was a problem. Now ready to complete the rescue, she wouldn't let us pull her aboard and as our overexcited passengers were watching all this and taking photographs, she would not tell us why. Brian and I were hanging from the outside of the railings, holding her by the wrists and so as quietly as I could I asked what the problem was, to which she hissed, "I'm fucking naked! Can you get a towel or something?" My crewmate and I just looked at each other dumbfounded before Brian, ever the gentleman, went to fetch his jacket. We fished her out and took her to the crew quarters for a hot drink. It transpired that the three of them had been fooling around in the rowboat and lost an oar. There being a breeze, the boat and oar had quickly drifted apart. After arguing who would swim for it, our Aussie sheilah stripped off and went after it, only to get cramp and further separated from her pals. She was quite a character with a veritable technicolour turn of phrase. For the record, she was not completely naked, but was wearing a very brief pair of panties, white lacy ones, if memory serves… happy days.

As the summer of 1973 drew to a close and with my fiancé and I having set a wedding date for the 1st December, I was frequently being reminded by my parents that I would need to find a "proper job". This began to cause me untold stress and so I simply put it to the back of my mind and decided to fall back on my Micawber like conviction that something would turn up.

Whilst I was blithely sleepwalking towards an uncertain future, my parents were one step ahead of me and began to seek a prospective career for me on my behalf. To this end, they paid a visit to a friend of theirs who happened to be a Police Sergeant in Grange-over-Sands and had a chat with him about a possible career in the constabulary. So enthusiastic were they about me getting a proper job, showing some responsibility etc that they had brought home an application form. It was presented to me over the dinner table, with strict instructions "that I at least fill it in and see what happens because look, you even get a house with the job."

I did not wish to disappoint them when they had clearly gone to so much trouble to get me off their hands. So, feigning as much interest as I could muster in the circumstances, I duly filled in the proffered application form and posted it off, secure in the knowledge that I had a trump card to play. It seemed to have escaped their minds, but not mine, that I was colour blind and that the constabulary would be less likely to welcome a colour blind bobby into its ranks, than a politician would be to take a lie detector test.

Some two weeks after posting my application, I was invited to sit the police entrance exam at Grange over sands Police Station (remember when we had Police Stations?). I passed with flying colours. Next came a request that I present myself for a formal interview and medical at Cumbria Police Headquarters, Carleton Hall, Penrith. I was not unduly concerned by this, they were to pay my travel expenses and provide me with lunch and I had never been to Penrith, so I thought what a smashing day out it was going to be.

The great day arrived and I found myself being interviewed by the Chief Constable, who enquired as to why I wished to join the force. Donning my most earnest and eager face, (I had been rehearsing for days using the bathroom mirror) I replied that it had been my foremost ambition, since leaving school. Also, that both my parents and myself would be most proud and honoured were I to secure a post. I swear I saw a moistening of his eyes as he swallowed, cleared his throat and declared, "Mr Nixon, you seem the very calibre of young man we are seeking to recruit." and then added, "You will be given a full medical examination, this will take place in Penrith, transport will be provided after lunch."

Our free meal was a grand affair. In fact my plate was so full from the serve-your- self buffet that I struggled to eat it in time to finish my two puddings. Afterwards, I and other fellow applicants were motored off to a doctor's surgery in the town where I was subjected to a very thorough examination indeed, the highlight of which for me was the eyesight test. I was shown various cards on which were multi-coloured dots and was asked what I could see. I should have been seeing numbers; however, all I could see was a version of what happens to your TV screen when you lose the signal.

Examinations completed, I and my eager companions were returned to Police HQ. Around mid afternoon I was summoned to the Chief Constables office to be informed whether I was to join the ranks of 'the boys in blue', or otherwise. As I approached his desk and was invited to sit, his decision was writ large across his face. I swear that once again his eyes were moist as he announced, "I am extremely sorry young man, but we are unable to offer you a position in the force." I swallowed hard and did my utmost to appear dismayed and pleaded "Why ever not sir? I am in good health and more than meet the height requirement." "Yes this is true", he replied, "but I am afraid you appear to be colour blind and that bans you from recruitment." I nodded wearily and was asked to let in the next candidate who I am sure made the grade because he looked just like that bastard who booked me, in Whitehaven in 1988, for having a brake light out. Upon arriving home from what had been a grand day out, my poor parents were totally underwhelmed by the news that, once again, I was to be regarded as an employment liability to yet another profession.

It was now nearly autumn. With the end of sailing on Windermere fast approaching, I was once again looking for a job but with a level of urgency I had not exercised before because also fast approaching, was my wedding on the 1st of December. Again, I was fortunate and found a job running the paint spray shop at a firm in Backbarrow called Tanco Engineering. The company assembled agricultural machinery, which was then sprayed with a cloying foul smelling enamel. This was almost impossible to remove from your hair or skin and clogged face masks very quickly. It was an extremely unpleasant and unhealthy work environment, but needs must when the devil drives.

The boss at Tanco was a guy named Tommy who brightened our days by singing constantly and tunelessly, all the while admonishing us for shortfalls in production. Mangling the lyrics to popular songs much to our amusement, some examples were: His version of *Green, Green Grass of Home* which went "The bold home town looks the same, as I step back from the game"; The Beatles *A Hard Day's Night* was rendered as, "It's been a hard day's night and I've been leaping on a log"; delving further into memory, *The Skye Boat Song* featured Larry the Lamb who was born to be king. The lads who had worked for him a while insisted that he did this intentionally. I always thought he had an affliction of some sort which made him as hard to listen to, as he was to work for. To laugh at him today would doubtless be considered a hate crime.

On the 1st December 1973, at the tender age of twenty, I was married to Fay at Pennington Church, just outside Ulverston. I was only granted three days leave from work and we spent our honeymoon at the Pennington Arms in Ravenglass. We had considered the Caribbean, but as Fay was very fair skinned and I was skint it seemed a sensible compromise. Our first home as a married couple was a small caravan next to my parents' bungalow in High Newton, which we made cosy and comfortable as we looked forward to our first Christmas as newlyweds.

The festive season was to be somewhat spoiled for me, as only two days before Christmas, I set myself on fire. As is still the custom today, a workforce will often decamp to the nearest public house to partake of a liquid lunch, prior to winding things up for the Yuletide break. In our instance, it was the Anglers Arms public house in Haverthwaite where we enjoyed a greatly extended lunch hour. We returned to our workplaces drunk as skunks to tidy things up before clocking off for the holiday shut down. A dirty spray gun is a frustration to use and I was always fastidious about cleaning mine, soaking the disassembled parts in paint thinners.

Afterwards, the thinners were decanted into a waste container to be used for burning masking tape and other rubbish in a 50 gallon drum out behind the factory. Having cleared my spray bay of waste and crammed it into the said drum, I went back to bring out what must have been over two gallons of used thinners, tipping it over the drum full of rubbish. Pleased with my efforts I took out my cigarettes, lit one and tossed the match into the waste upon which the vapour from the thinners ignited, with the resulting explosion blowing me clean off my feet. As I lay on my back, now both drunk and stunned as well, I saw a huge mushroom plume of flames and debris erupt skywards. I had no time to marvel at this spectacle though because my overalls were on fire! In my drunken state I had spilled thinners down my legs which were now well ablaze. Upon hearing the explosion, two of my workmates came running out and rolled me in a muddy puddle, extinguishing the flames and without doubt saving me from very severe burns. As it was, I spent my Christmas day with blistered and bandaged legs, too traumatised even to be in the same room when they set the pudding alight.

After a winter of spraying paint I was ready for a change once again. On a sunny April morning, myself and another guy, also John, downed our tools, went to the pub and then signed on for what would be for me, (though I did not know it) my final season on the lake. You could be forgiven for thinking that a summer working on the lake in such idyllic surroundings would be less than fraught with danger. However, once again I found yet another way to kill myself, albeit a more banal one, this time by drowning.

It was strictly frowned upon, but approaching docking at a pier and before the boat was tied up alongside, some of us would jump the gap. It could be several feet between the landing and the stern deck railings. This would allow us a little extra time to race to the pier café to pick up our pre-ordered and plated up lunch. On the day in question I did just such a thing, but on this occasion my foot slipped off the rail, hampering my launch somewhat. I made contact with Ambleside pier chest first and was scrabbling at the

With barman Geoff Higgs MV Teal 1974

concrete (think cartoon cat), before plunging feet first into the lake, between the landing stage and the MV Teal. This situation was extremely hazardous for me as (A) we had gone astern to dock (that's backwards to the non nautical) and the propeller wash was driving water under the pier; (B) at 21 years of age I could not swim a bloody stroke!

The sensation I experienced was akin, I imagine, to that of being thrown into a giant washing machine, but I recall having the presence of mind to hold my breath in the hope of maintaining some degree of buoyancy. It is a known fact (allegedly), that you need to sink for the third time before you drown. So, I reasoned that if I could grab something upon surfacing for the first or second time, then I might survive this latest peril to my young life. I seemed to be submerged for an eternity and surfacing did not seem in prospect. I don't recall seeing my chaotic life flash before my eyes, but I did at one point experience a brief calmness, an acceptance almost, about what was happening to me. I have spoken to others about their own near drowning experiences and most describe the brief loss of urgency, and the same emotion I felt. I wonder if this is because we spend the first nine months of our lives in a liquid environment. We survivors all agree however that such feelings are short lived and as with birth, the overriding desire is to get out, get dried off and see what the rest of your life has to offer!

I surfaced just inches from being swept under the concrete apron beneath the pier, which without a doubt would have been the death of me had it happened. My rescuers found me clinging (and cursing), to an old wooden pile. I spent the next two weeks off work with a bone chip in my wrist joint and a cracked sternum; the latter of which can cause discomfort at times, still to this day.

When I cast my mind back I was approaching the end of the sailing season on Windermere without a care in the world: no permanent job prospects; a caravan home; a bemused wife and parents who were at their wits end with me. Something had to give. Whilst I was unfazed by this situation (something always turned up), my parents were not. Over the dinner table one evening I was presented with an application form for Her Majesty's Prison Service, freshly clipped from the pages of the Daily Mirror. My parents were most enthusiastic: "and look, they even give you a house!", "at least fill it in, the wages seem good and it's a job for life, with a pension." Bless their hearts they were so excited about the prospect of "our John getting a proper job", that I thought, why not fill it in, keep them happy, no harm in that. I filled in the application, posted it, and went off with Fay for a holiday in Jersey, without giving the matter a second thought.

Upon arriving home just over a week later, my mother met us at the door gleefully waving a letter addressed to me. It transpired it was an invitation for me to sit the entrance exam for the Prison Service. At this time I had begun making a little money, carrying out car body repairs and resprays in our family garage and enjoying my evenings with pals in the Crown Hotel. With my abject failure to be recruited by the police firmly fixed in my mind I thought, "Why not, it's a day out?" So, on the 15th November 1974 I travelled to Her Majesty's Prison Preston, secure and happy in the belief that I could and would once again ruin the plans of any well meaning folk who would attempt to saddle me with "a proper job"!

As I left for my 'proper job' Dad became permanent skipper of the MV Swan.
Seen here on her bridge with his friend and first mate the late Alan Hudson.

CHAPTER FIVE

Welcome to the Machine -
Pink Floyd

My first and overwhelming impression of HMP Preston was how grim and forbidding it looked with its high walls, razor wire and huge gates. Putting any reservations aside, I rang the bell. A small hatch in the gate opened to reveal an equally grim and forbidding Prison Officer who enquired as to what business I had at the establishment. I informed him that I was reporting to sit the Prison Service examination and be interviewed, to which he replied with a wry smile, "So you want to be a screw, eh son? Well, come on lad, come on in."

I was taken to a small room adjacent to the prison's administration building where in due course and along with several other candidates I sat the entrance examination. Approximately an hour afterwards, following the marking of our papers we were split into two groups. The larger of which had passed the exam and a smaller group who were dismissed.

By now it was lunchtime and I was about to experience the gastronomic challenge that is Prison mess food. I was bitterly disappointed. It was not a patch on the food at Police Headquarters and it was a set portion with a very poor pudding. What I did not realise was that I would be eating prison staff mess food of varying quality for the next three decades.

Following this less than inspiring repast, we chosen ones were trooped off to the prison hospital to undergo our medical examinations, giving me the chance to see a bit more of this grim edifice. The more I saw of it, the less I liked the bloody look of it. The medical we underwent was most thorough and of course the highlight for me personally was the eyesight test. Out came the charts with all the letters, which I read perfectly but I could scarcely contain my excitement when I was presented with the cards covered in coloured dots, which were to be quite literally my 'get out of jail free' cards. Having been shown several of these cards - all the while cocking my head this way and that, squinting and shaking my head - I was informed that my examination was complete and was sent to sit in a waiting area, whilst the rest of the group had theirs.

Golly, we were an excited bunch as we were taken to meet the Prison Governor for a short interview and a yay or nay with regard to our appointment. My fellows were excited by the fact that perhaps a career awaited them behind fifteen foot high walls and razor wire. I was excited because I had enjoyed another grand day out with lunch (albeit a poor one) at no expense to myself and kept my family happy into the bargain.

I recall that I was the last man to be interviewed and I was asked why I wanted to join the Prison Service. I informed the Governor and Chief Officer of my desolation at having been denied a place in the police force, adding that this was my earnest attempt to forge a career in uniform, to ensure secure employment and a good standard of living for myself and my wife. The Governor and Chief Officer looked at one another and then beaming, the Governor looked at me and announced, "Congratulations Mr Nixon! We are pleased to offer you a post. Subject to one month's induction here at HMP Preston, you will, if considered suitable, be sent to our training academy in Wakefield, Yorkshire to undertake eight weeks training."

Try to imagine the sickening jolt you feel when the dentist tells you "I'm sorry, but those four teeth will have to come out." The feeling when you realise that somewhere you have lost your wallet with all your credit and debit cards; well multiply that by ten and you still wouldn't come close to the sickening jolt that this news gave me. I just stared at him blankly, until he enquired "Do you have any questions Mr Nixon?" I replied that I did not. However, I said that I thought it only fair (and to avoid any disappointment or inconvenience for myself or the Prison Service in the future) if I pointed out that something may have been overlooked during my medical examination. "Oh?" he said, before opening my file, peering at it and then enquiring what the nature of my affliction might be. I announced that I was in fact colour blind, to which once again he beamed and said "Let me put your mind at rest; it is not a requirement of this service that you have full colour vision and we would like you to report here at 10.00am sharp on the 15th of December." In my stunned and distressed state I could think of nothing to say and so simply replied "Thank you Sir."

As we successful applicants were being escorted back to the prison's gates by a Principal Officer, I said to him, "I am severely colour blind and they would not allow me to join the police force." He put his arm across my shoulder in a somewhat avuncular and understanding way (this would never happen again in all my long service) and said, "Don't worry about it my lad, we only have white uns, black uns, brown uns and the occasional yeller un, but we treat em all't same."

I recall nothing of the train journey home, but have a most vivid recollection of the near hysteria exhibited by my family at the news that "Our John's got a proper job." As for me, well you might as well have cancelled Christmas and trepidation does not come close to describing my feelings about what I had got myself into…

So it came to pass that on the appointed date and at the appointed time, I did, though not without a little apprehension, present myself at the gates of HMP Preston, Ribbleton Lane. Along with my fellow recruits I was given a lapel badge, a notebook and a pen, and officially became a P.O.U.T or Prison Officer Under Training (the Prison Service adores acronyms.). Next on our agenda was a visit to the administration building where we were required to sign the Official Secrets Act before leaving the main prison for lunch in the Officer's Mess, situated just outside the gates to the left of the gate lodge. It was run by a member of staff and a trustee 'inmate'. A prisoner in such a position was known as a 'red band' and one was worn on their arm to signify that they were in a position of trust.

As the distance from home was too great to facilitate easy daily travel for me, I, along with two more recruits, was to lodge in the establishment's 'Bachelor Quarters', again outside the prison and above the Officers Mess. I liked my two fellow lodgers straight away. Fred was from Barrow-in-Furness and Joe was from Carlisle. Following a mediocre lunch we took our bags and went to move into our respective rooms, but this was not to be straightforward at all. Upon going to the stairs area at the back of the Mess to access our rooms we found that there were no stairs. The rear of the Mess really was a mess. It resembled a building site. Provided for our ascent was a builder's ladder, which was lashed into place approximately where the staircase had once been. We had been informed by the Training Principal Officer that work was being done and that the accommodation was somewhat basic, but this was not at all what we had expected. We looked at each other, then back at the ladder and then back at each other again before Fred murmured, "They have got to be taking the piss!" upon which all three of us began laughing uncontrollably. It served as the perfect ice breaker for us and we never looked back as a trio from that point on.

Having scaled the aforementioned ladder we found our allocated rooms, which turned out to be comfortable, if not luxurious. After stowing our luggage we did what any sensible trio would do in the circumstances; we went off on a pub crawl up Ribbleton Lane and rounded our evening off with a portion each of fish and chips from the Happy Haddock. Returning to our temporary home it's fair to say that we found the ladder more of a challenge than we had initially.

Down our ladder we went the next morning and after being booked through the gate lodge at 07.00 hrs, we made our way to the wings where we were to be paired up with the officers who would act as our mentors for the day. The wings of our old Victorian prisons run out from a central point known sensibly

47

enough as The Centre where the Chief Officer and senior ranks were situated in a main office there. Preston's wings were three landings high with steel netting between each landing to prevent prisoners attempting or committing suicide, by jumping from the landings to the ground floor.

From The Centre, officers were allocated to their respective landing to begin the day with the most important task of the day, the roll check. I was sent with my mentor and two other officers up onto the 'threes' to observe. Two officers would work their way down each side of the landing counting prisoners. When this was completed and sufficient time had elapsed, a call would come up from The Centre in a parade ground voice, "How many on the ones?" The numbers would be shouted back down followed by the twos and threes landings. All numbers would be added up. If subsequently announced correct and collated with the numbers from the other two wings, without discrepancies, it results in the roll being pronounced correct. The prison day could begin. "Roll correct" was followed by the next call from The Centre, "Unlock". The two officers would make their way down each side of the landing, unlocking all the cell doors. Meanwhile, an officer stayed at the end of the landing with access to an alarm bell in case of any violence or other problems which might require the deployment of additional staff. On this, my first morning under training, my mentor and I were covering the alarm bell and observing these proceedings. I was quite overawed by the totally alien situation I found myself in, this was not the Lake Windermere Steamers.

With all doors unlocked, no prisoner appeared until my mentor shouted "By your doors", upon which all the prisoners emerged from their cells, each carrying a plastic chamber pot containing their nights excrement and urine. The next command, which was "Slop out", instructed all prisoners to file quietly to an area known as the recess, which was fitted with huge Belfast type sinks into which each man emptied his pot. In the confines of the wing and with this taking place on the landings below as well, the stench was overpowering; I can clearly recall that l was trying not to gag as it drifted over me like a fog.

48

All prisoners in the 1970's were subject to far more discipline than is exercised in today's prisons. Dress was important; each man was in a prison grey jacket and trousers with a striped shirt and tie. There was an requirement to maintain a clean and tidy cell and make up a military style bed pack before leaving the wing for work, or labour as it was known, each morning. Being clean shaven was another requirement, unless the prisoner had a beard upon reception. Growing a beard whilst in custody would constitute a change of appearance and thereby be deemed a security risk.

Also considered a security risk if uncontrolled, were razor blades. To avoid them being used as a weapon, or a means of self injury, they were handed out each morning before breakfast from a board which had each man's name and cell number on it. The razor was to be returned as soon as he had shaved. These were the days of the old style safety razors. However, in later years the Prison Service would go on to hand out disposable razors, as and when requested. This type of razor is very easy to take apart and remove the blade, or blades. These could be used in three main ways: as a means to cause self harm; placement where officers would be likely to conduct a finger search, such as pipe lagging; or to create a weapon by setting them into a melted toothbrush handle. From the time that prisoners began using this weapon it evolved to one where instead of a single blade, there would be two or three set side by side. These carefully spaced blades created a deep, triple and horrible wound which was very difficult to stitch and a nasty scar would be the result as a reminder of an unpaid debt or the consequences of being a 'grass' etc.

Breakfast came next that morning, with officers controlling a steady flow of prisoners down to the hotplates on the ground floor, or the "ones" as they were known The men would pick up their breakfast on a sectioned stainless steel tray and take it back to their cells to eat, being locked in once again until it was time for labour. Any meal time meant extra vigilance from officers; grudges could be aired and fights break out when prisoners were out of their cells in numbers. Quite often fists would not be the first weapon of choice, but rather the steel meal tray, the edge of which I have seen cause facial injuries down to the bone, before these were done away with and replaced by plastic plates and bowls.

Until the 1980's officers in most of Britain's prisons would carry out a roll check, slop out the wing, breakfast the prisoners, relock and then go off duty for a breakfast break themselves. This left the next contingent of officers who came on duty an hour later at 08.00 hrs to progress the rest of the regime. Dirty breakfast trays went out for washing and prisoner movement commenced to their respective places of work. Having completed our first brief stint on the landings that morning, I met Fred and Joe in the mess for breakfast and we took a table in the corner, feeling very much like the rookies we were. "Well," said Joe, "that was an experience!" Fred, who would go on to prove he had a stomach of cast iron, sniffed the air and announced "I'm bloody starving, that grub smells good." Then turning to me and seeing a less than enthusiastic expression on my face he enquired "What's up with you Nico?" (This nickname stuck right through my service). I replied that in all honesty all I could smell was shit.

I spent the rest of the morning in one of the prison's workshops watching prisoners sewing mailbags, the heavy canvas type used by the Post Office for bulk loading mail. It was riveting stuff. All the bags had to be sewn with very strong thread with eight stitches to the inch and had four D-rings sewn onto the neck. Before being used, the thread had to be waxed by hand. A prisoner who usually sat in a corner would draw lengths of it through a block of wax, all the while in a sort of semi coma at the boredom of the task. By the mid 70's things were slowly changing in our jails and a radio was allowed to be played in the workshop whilst the prisoners worked. This was something new. However, at the time I joined the prison service smoking and talking to each other were largely forbidden or discouraged in work situations in our older prisons though it would not be long before rules such as this would finally be relaxed.

I don't recall what we dined upon that lunchtime, on our first day at Preston, but I well remember that it almost did a curtain call that afternoon. In my ignorance it had never occurred to me that I might be required to exert myself in a strenuous manner at this early stage and so I was horrified when we were marched off to the prison gymnasium, for our first Physical Training session. I had not visited a gym or worn shorts since I left school and I knew that what was to ensue would not be a pleasant experience for me. Immediately I did not like the look or the sound of the gym instructor at all. He was ex military and it is fair to say that had you cut the top off his head you would have seen written right through his body "British Army Physical Training Instructor" just like a stick of Blackpool rock. We began with a fifteen minute run to warm up (I was warm enough already), followed by circuit training. The only circuit I knew was an electrical one and if you will allow me the pun, this one was a bloody shocker.

Christmas came and went and over the four weeks spent at HMP Preston we three were gently schooled in how and how not to interact with prisoners. We gained some fitness (not so gently) and began to learn the basics of prison rules and how the various establishments functioned across the prison estate. All this was in preparation for our eight weeks basic training at HM Prison Training College, Aberford Road, Wakefield, Yorkshire.

Following a period of leave, myself, Joe and Fred made the journey down to Wakefield in Fred's car and that is how we three travelled for the two months we were in post there. I think we were given weekend leave once a fortnight, but my memory may not serve me correctly. The Training College was a very modern establishment with single rooms of a very high standard, which could be reached without a ladder, a large and comfortable lecture theatre and good mess facilities with great food aplenty; now this was more like it.

I found the coursework hard at first. I had never been able to give classroom work my full attention for long, but this experience taught me a degree of self discipline in that respect.

Prison Officers Training School, Aberford Rd, Wakefield. (I am fifth from left, middle row)

We were schooled in the laws and rules by which prison establishments functioned and the curriculum involved a fair amount of essay writing and open forum with our course tutors. Even having gained a little fitness during our first four weeks at our respective prisons, initially some of us found the gym work pretty tough: the dreaded circuit training, running, being taught restraint and self defence techniques. The self defence stuff was a tad late for me. I should have been shown that stuff before I was sent to secondary school..

Our tutors were all of Principal Officer rank and at the head of the Training College was the Governor, Deputy Governor and Chief Officer. The rank structure at this time throughout the service was: Governor, Deputy Governor, Chief Officer, Principal Officer, Senior Officer and the basic grade Officer. However, around the time that I joined, an additional rank was added, one of Assistant Governor. These were carefully selected and recruited men who joined the service at that rank. A good number of them were University educated and would find themselves working at wing level dealing with Governor grade issues alongside the wing's Principal Officer. During those early days it was easy at times to detect a degree of resentment at their presence from the older prison Governors. Governors who had perhaps spent years of hard work ascending the promotion ladder from uniform duties and having been through several postings to get there.

It is to be remembered that I am writing of the Prison Service in the mid 1970's with capital punishment (hanging) having only been abolished in 1969. The last men to be hanged were Gwynne Owen Evans at HMP Strangeways and Peter Anthony Allen at HMP Walton on the 13th August 1964. Ruth Ellis was the last woman to be hanged in 1955 at HMP Holloway. All avenues to reinstating the death penalty were closed in 1998. The House of Commons voted to ratify the 6th protocol of the European Convention on Human Rights, prohibiting capital punishment except "in time of war or imminent threat of war", thereby prohibiting the death penalty, though interestingly, technically only while Britain was part of the European Union.

More than one of our tutors had carried out 'death cell duty', or acted as Capital Charge Officers, which was the official title for the duty. A week prior to the condemned man's execution, eight officers would be drawn from another prison. Six of whom would spend eight hour shifts, 24 hours a day with him and would be paid extra for it. Just before the man's execution the additional two officers, who the prisoner had never met, would take over. It was felt that it might be somewhat traumatic for any of the initial six who had come to know the prisoner as a person, rather than a case file.

We questioned our tutors closely about the experience and they described playing cards and chess, or just chatting to the condemned man. They perhaps wrote letters for him (illiteracy was common among the prison population right up to my retirement) and at the parting of ways the prisoner would often shake hands with them and thank them for their company. It worried me then and still does now that these seemingly decent and well balanced men could be involved so closely in the execution process, but quite obviously be totally unaffected by the experience, indeed they spoke about it as simply being part of their duties at the time.

Perhaps we are all capable of more than we think just so long as it is state sanctioned?

Wakefield offered a varied and vibrant social life for us trainees. For the single lads the pretty girls from the Nurses Training College were a draw and for the rest of us, dozens of bars and entertainment venues beckoned. I was appointed Entertainments Officer for my section which involved obtaining concession tickets for various clubs, one of which was the famous, though now closed, Batley Variety Club. This venue always hosted the big names in entertainment, I remember seeing Howard Keel there; what a voice. The most popular night out of all though (an eye opener to a lad from a small village), was Heppys Fish and Strip. This was a fish and chip shop at the front, with a bar and strip joint out the back. You bought your fish and chips (reduced price to us) and in you went. The girls were all quite lovely, but the star of the show every time was a generously proportioned lady who would dance naked with a giant fluffy teddy bear. Her stage name was Petite Fleur, which I think means little flower. She was not little and she was certainly not a shrinking violet. As soon as she appeared there would be rapturous applause and much stomping of feet as she began to disrobe and gyrate wildly…….. the chips were good too.

After five weeks of our fun and games it was time for more serious concerns. Top of that list was where we were to be posted following the completion of training. How a prison was categorised by the prisoners it held would influence that choice. After the escape from Wormwood Scrubs by the spy George Blake on 22th October 1966, a report was submitted by Earl Mountbatten into how Category A and B high risk prisoners were incarcerated. This was followed in 1968 by the Radzinowicz report which made recommendations on the regime for long term prisoners in maximum security conditions. The categories of prisoner were defined as:

Category A – Prisoners who in no circumstances should be allowed to escape either because of security considerations affecting spies, or because of the fact that their violent behaviour is such that members of the public, or the police, would be in danger of their lives if they were to get out.

Category B – Prisoners for whom the very high expenditure on the most modern escape barriers may not be justified, but who ought to be kept in secure conditions.

Category C – Prisoners who lack the resources and will to make escape attempts, but have not the stability to be kept in conditions where there is no barrier to escape.

Category D – Prisoners deemed suitable for open conditions where no escape barrier exists.

Having viewed these definitions of establishment and being granted three choices of a posting, for me it was a no brainer. Maximum security establishments were firmly off my list of considerations; it was Category C or D for me.

My three choices were HMP Lancaster Castle (close to home), HMP Haverigg (also close to home) and top of my list was HMP Bela River, a category D open prison near Milnthorpe; not too much stress to be endured there I reasoned. So I made my submissions and awaited the outcome. One week later we entered our course room to find an envelope on each of our desks. This was it. Off back up north to a nice cushy category D nick in a quiet backwater. However, this was not to be. Upon opening my posting notification, the words HMP Gartree meant nothing to me at all and I thought that there must have been some kind of mistake. I turned to the guy next to me and said "Where the hell is Gartree?" to which he replied "Woah! Nice one Nico you've hit the jackpot there. It's a big modern maximum security nick down in the Midlands. You must have heard of it. They had that massive riot there in 1972."

Maximum security? Midlands? Riot? I didn't think so. I was having none of that and when we were informed that we could appeal against our postings decisions I did so straight away. The next day I was presented to the Chief Officer who enquired as to why I was not happy with my posting. I told him that with respect I had requested three postings, all in the North West, any one of which I would have been happy with. He looked at me perplexed and said "But surely Officer Nixon, you do realise that HMP Gartree is north west of HMP Brixton don't you?" The implied threat was unmistakable; HMP Gartree or it's the big smoke for you my lad, you're in uniform now. , thus chastened I thanked him and went off to phone my wife with the good news...

For those of us who would be posted into maximum security institutions the final part of our training became a good deal more specific. Senior members of uniformed staff were attached to the college to coach us in what to expect and how these very different regimes functioned. They were excellent in this task and gave us all the confidence we needed before we undertook our 12 months probation in our respective establishments. Also, they encouraged us to feel a little special in that we had been deemed suitable to be selected for such work. I just felt that I had been stitched up.

With our training almost at an end it naturally fell to me as Entertainments Officer to organise an end of course bash. No canvassing was necessary. It had of course to be Heppy's. So it was that over a fine feed of fish and chips and many beers that we bade a somewhat sad farewell to Wakefield, Heppy's, Petite Fleur and her fluffy teddy.

I travelled down to take up post at Gartree in late March, making the journey in my battered old mini. It was my first real experience of motorway driving, which I found quite nerve wracking. On arrival I found that I was one of I think twelve probationary officers, most of whom were older than myself and with more than one of them who had come to the service after leaving one of the armed forces. After a formal welcome by the prison's Principal Training Officer we were directed down to the bachelor accommodation and mess. Those who were not from the area were allocated rooms, not as well appointed as our rooms at Wakefield, but once again thankfully easily reached without a builder's ladder. We made our way that first night to the adjacent Prison Officers Club where we were welcomed into the fold with a great deal of good natured leg pulling and much proffered advice from the

Trying to look the part in my new and proper job

old hands, all of it welcome. As we made our way back to our rooms the prison was an impressive sight, with its huge walls and high mast lighting rendering the whole area around it as bright as daylight. Ultra modern in every respect and the polar opposite of HMP Preston, whatever our posting brought us we all agreed that it was going to be interesting.

Next morning after breakfast in the mess, we made our way into the jail to complete whatever admin was required and the morning was rounded off by the issue of our uniforms. I recall being measured for it at Wakefield, but it seems that these were merely a rough guide, as when I got to my room and began to try it on, the assembled pieces of it varied wildly from roomy, to very snug. Fortunately the other lads found theirs to be the same and so we dumped the whole lot on my bed and by trial and error found a full outfit that was a reasonable fit. Luckily, we all varied in size a bit.

Suitably decked out now, we went for our mess lunch and arrived to the sound of hymns being pounded out on a piano by a very large and forbidding looking geordie officer who ran the kitchen. This guy was an ex-miner, with hands like shovels and no catering skills whatsoever. To criticise his attempts at cooking was to incur a terrible wrath; better to just eat what you could and say nothing. I remember eating one of his salads to the strains of The Old Rugged Cross: an ungrated rectangle of cheese; two unsliced tomatoes; an unsliced egg with small pieces of shell stuck to it and lettuce, which still played host to the wildlife that had once called it home. I have forgotten his name, but not his food.

We were each given a member of staff to shadow for our first few weeks as we gradually familiarised ourselves with the establishment, its industries and its security systems. Gartree was laid out in the form of an H; four wings, three landings high with extremely secure cells for prisoners, offices for staff and food service areas. The centre corridor housed a staff tea room, the Chief Officer's office, staff detail office and a room with four members of uniform staff, on permanent standby to deploy to any trouble on the wings or in the workshops. As prisoners would occasionally barricade themselves in their cells, this team was equipped with a hydraulic jack with which to force entry.

At the heart of the prison was the control room situated in a sterile area from which our radio net operated. The whole establishment was monitored constantly by overhead cameras both inside and outside the perimeter wall. This wall was capped by a domed structure for its entire length, designed to prevent the use of a rope and grapple. Inside the wall was a high wire fence topped with copious amounts of razor wire. Between these two barriers a constant staff patrol was maintained. In addition to this, the internal fence was equipped with an ultra sensitive geophone alarm system. It meant that staff in the central control room could detect any interference with it, by monitoring columns of light on a display panel next to the camera monitors. So sensitive was this system that it registered the footsteps of patrolling staff. Gartree was indeed a very modern establishment and a world apart from our old Victorian jails.

This was a time when it had been decided at the highest level that a policy of dispersal should be adopted for maximum security prisons. Less serious offenders would be dispersed to form part of their population. The thinking being that this would prove a stabilising influence overall and so prisons like Gartree were known as dispersal prisons.

Gradually we newcomers began to take up our duties independently, both on our designated landings and as a presence in the various workshops to ensure order, and the safety of the civilian instructors who ran them. In a large workshop such as the woollen weaving section, three members of staff would be in post, one sat at each end and one patrolling between the two. It was tedious stuff, but you needed to have your eyes everywhere. I recall in later months finding a twelve foot long woollen sock in the receiving hopper under a machine. I wonder what that was for. Obviously there was skulduggery afoot.

I had been allocated a prison quarter on Coleman Road in the village of Fleckney, some six miles away from the prison. It was a fairly new build and my wife and I were delighted with both the house and the village. The trip to and from the jail took approximately fifteen minutes each way, which meant that those of us who lived out there could travel home and have a thirty minute lunch break out of our permitted one hour.

During the time I spent in post at Gartree, staff routinely worked seven days a week and the shifts were usually the same: on duty at 07.00 hrs; breakfast break for an hour at 08.00 hrs; back on duty; one hour for lunch. I think we had a 45 minute dinner break around 16.00 hrs and finishing after lockup at 21.30 hrs, was a 14 ½ hour day. It seems incredible now, but I once worked 78 of these shifts, one after the other and that was not at all unusual.

As one can imagine it was hard on family life and a stressful time too as the Irish Republican Army were carrying out a vicious bombing campaign in Britain. We were holding several Irish terrorists and would go on to see some of the most notorious come through our gates as time progressed. Each morning we would check our cars before leaving for work and our wives were given explicit instructions not to open any mail, packages or otherwise. It was felt that as they had been in Ireland, prison staff would be considered legitimate targets by the IRA.

Once you begin work in the prison service you quickly begin to assimilate and use a whole new terminology; prisoners become 'cons'; staff are 'screws'; sex case prisoners are 'nonces'; informants are 'grasses'; safe breakers are 'peter men' etc. 'Con' of course is an abbreviation of convict. 'Screw' is thought to have originated back in the old treadmill days of hard labour, when an officer would turn a screw to increase the effort required to turn the mill. The term 'nonce' refers to a sexual offender or anyone who has committed an offence which is considered a crime outside the understanding of the general criminal fraternity, hence a nonsense crime. The term 'grass', as most know, is a title given to any informant, but 'peter man' is an interesting one. It harks back to the days when the safe crackers would mix their own explosives, one of the main components being saltpetre. It was still in common usage to describe those who blew safes during my days at Gartree.

The prison service training school prepared me for many things. However, dealing and coping with the harsher side of prison life can only be achieved through hard experience. I was about four or five months into my posting to Gartree and on landing duty one morning when I was approached by a young prisoner who asked me for a tin of boot polish. I went with him to the landing store room and gave him a tin. He asked if he could have two. I saw no reason not to give him a second one and nothing in his manner suggested anything untoward, so off he went back to his cell. Whilst I was talking to a colleague some thirty minutes later, we were interrupted by a loud crashing and banging further down the landing. It was clear that someone was wrecking their cell, or 'smashing up', as it is known by staff and prisoners alike. It transpired that it was the prisoner to whom I had given the boot polish and he had partially barricaded his door before smashing every breakable item in his cell. We could get no response from him. Forcing his door we found him slumped in a corner in a pool of blood refusing to speak to us and with ragged gashes to both wrists. On the walls of is cell he had written in boot polish, "You fucking bastards are to blame for this", then split the lid of one of the tins and used it to slash his wrists. We wrapped his arms in clean towels and off he was taken to the prison's hospital, whilst I was left to file and submit a report to our wing Senior Officer. After reading it he looked up and without the trace of a smile on his face enquired, "Had you at no point thought that the prisoner might try to polish himself off?" Black humour served us well in upsetting times and over the years I made an art form of it.

I am often asked if I come across the Kray twins during my time in maximum security; I did not. However, I did have three members of their 'firm' on the wing where I worked. Chris and Tony Lambrianou and Ronald 'Ronnie' Bender were serving 15 years each for their involvement in the murder of Jack 'The Hat' McVitie. Following the murder they were to dispose of the body and so they put his corpse in the boot of his car, drove it south of the Thames River and dumped it on the territory of their rival gang, the Richardson's. To avoid a gang war the Kray twins had the body removed, resulting in the persistence of a very strong rumour that Jack ended up as pig food on an Essex farm.

Interestingly, we were also locking up Charlie Richardson too, so one would have expected some friction because of old rivalries. However, they rubbed along together okay. Charlie and his brother Eddie ran the aforementioned Richardson gang from a scrap yard in Peckham. The outfit was into just about every sort of gangland crime there was and earned a fearsome reputation for torture. On one occasion a member who collected protection money for the gang was caught after pocketing the money and spending it at the dog track; something he was previously warned against. He was taken to a warehouse near Tower Bridge and nailed to the floor for nearly two days, with six-inch nails through his feet, receiving regular visits from gang members who would urinate on him.

Often the gang would hold mock trials where a transgressor would be hauled up in front of 'Judge' Charlie who would decide on a suitable punishment. This could include: severe flogging; cigarette burns; nailing to the floor with six inch nails; having toes removed with bolt croppers and being given electric shocks until the victim was unconscious. The shocks would be administered using a hand cranked generator and the victim would be sat in cold water to further enhance the charge with the terminals attached to the man's genitals. Always present at proceedings was the gang's enforcer 'Mad' Frankie Frazier, whose personal speciality was tearing out teeth with a pair of pliers. This process of trial followed by torture was known as "Taking a shirt from Charlie" because of his habit of giving each victim a clean shirt to return home in, since the one they arrived in was usually covered in blood. Following many criminal adventures the Richardson brothers were found guilty in 1967 of fraud, extortion, assault and grievous bodily harm. Charlie was sentenced to 25 years and Eddie 15 years; their reign of terror was over.

By the time I joined the service, prisons were beginning to have to deal with an altogether different type of prisoner in the form of convicted IRA terrorists, who were proving dangerous and very disruptive. These men considered themselves to be 'freedom fighters' and as such political prisoners, held unjustly by the British penal system. A good number of disaffected prisoners, though not Irish, would attach themselves as sympathisers and engage in disruptive and subversive behaviour along with them.

On the 21st November 1974 and less than a month before I joined the Prison Service, two public houses in Birmingham, the Tavern in the Town and the Mulberry Bush, were bombed by the IRA with horrendous consequences. 21 people died and 182 were injured; the majority of the victims were between the ages of 17 and 30. In the wake of this atrocity six men were arrested whilst trying to leave the country to attend an IRA man's funeral in Northern Ireland. They were to become known as The Birmingham Six. They were Hugh Callaghan, Patrick Hill, Gerard Hunter, Richard Mcllkenny, William Power and John Walker. From the outset they protested their innocence. Finally, in 1991 they had their convictions quashed on appeal. After serving 16 years in prison, it was agreed that they had been forced into making false confessions, through severe physical and psychological abuse. At the time the IRA denied responsibility for the bombings and blamed a possible rogue element. No warnings were given before hand and the bombs were very large. 30lbs of nitroglycerin surrounded by shards of metal were packed into a holdall, clearly with the intention of causing carnage, which is exactly what happened. The six were separated throughout the prison system and we held Hunter and I think Power, both on my wing. I never saw either of them associate themselves with any of the IRA elements, their hangers on, nor engage in any disruptive or subversive behaviour. I have come to believe this pointed to an unsafe and wrongful conviction. In 2001 each of the six men were paid between £840,000 and £1.2 million in compensation, though it leaves a bitter taste to this day when I think that nobody has ever been convicted of that heinous crime, they simply got away with a large scale massacre of innocents and it seems unlikely now that we will ever know who was responsible.

Whilst the IRA prisoners gave us headaches enough, it was those who were on the fringe of them that most often gave us the most problems. One of them was a tiny bloke called Day. At only about six and a half stone he was always kicking off. One day I was part of a two man team who had been sent to remove him from his cell, after he had caused a problem at the food server. We were to take him to the segregation unit, but he was screaming blue murder and having none of it. About two minutes into the altercation he tried to dart between the two of us. Seeing me trying to block the door he promptly took my legs out from underneath me, cracking my head on the door frame and ran off down the landing, only to be cornered and captured by staff from the landing below. I had learned a lesson. It's not the dog that's in the fight; it's the fight that's in the dog.

Given that Gartree was one of the most secure prisons in the UK, with full strength dog patrols and state of the art surveillance systems, the regime there for prisoners was fairly relaxed when compared to that of HMP Preston. However, there were two types of prisoner for whom extra security measures were necessary. These were category A and category E men who were escorted everywhere by a member of staff. For each one there was a book which was to move with them. It was filled out with time of leaving the wing or workshop and handed over to have the place and time logged in at the arrival point. The category E men were prisoners who had or were suspected of trying to make an escape attempt. Bright yellow stripes down the leg of their prison issue grey trousers and yellow patches on their jackets made them highly visible to staff at all times.

Food was brought from the main kitchen which was situated on an upper level in the centre of the prison and brought to all four wings to be served from hotplates. All manner of diets - many contrived, I am sure - were catered for and the standard and variety of food served was generally quite good. Alongside the food server were two water boilers and prisoners would draw water from them to make tea in their large plastic jugs. As with many everyday items in prison, boiling water was weaponised from time to time and used as a means to settle a score, or a bad debt. Known as prison napalm, a syrupy mixture of sugar and boiling water not only scolds, but sticks causing severe injury. Two incidents spring to mind.

In the first, I was sat at the back of the communal television room one afternoon when I saw a prisoner entering with what I took to be a jug of tea. About five or ten minutes later one of the men sat at the front of the room must have wound his foot around the TV cable and yanked the plug out. As the room was plunged into darkness, save for the emergency light above my head, a scream went up from the middle of the seating area and a man leapt to his feet. It transpired that he had been the recipient of a jug of hot sugar water straight into his lap. I pushed the alarm bell and seconds later additional staff were on the scene to clear the room and take the victim to the prison hospital. Luckily and incredibly it seemed the mixture, though hot enough to cause a light blistering, did not cause the usual terrible burns and scarring suffered from such attacks. As is usually the case, no one knew who did it and the scolded man wasn't telling. I suspected, though could not prove it, that it was the man I saw enter with his jug. However, given that the sugar/water mix was not sufficiently hot as to cause more serious injury it is entirely plausible that the man's assailant had entered a little earlier as most prisoners carried jugs of tea to the tv rooms and it may have escaped my attention.

The second incident occurred one lunch time at the food server. A violent argument had broken out between two prisoners, which staff believed they had successfully defused. This was not the case. Some minutes later both men once again confronted one another, but this time each was holding a jug of boiling water and both clearly intent on throwing them. No one could believe their eyes when a young officer quickly and bravely (?) put himself between the two combatants and began to try and defuse the situation, as the rest of us held our breaths. It took some time to bring the standoff to an end but after a tense few minutes the two prisoners were separated and taken to the segregation unit to be placed on Governor's report. Afterwards someone said to the officer "What the hell were you thinking putting yourself in that situation?", "I didn't think!" was the reply. Then when the wing assistant Governor praised him for the impulsive and brave action he had taken and the way he had talked the men down he said, "It seemed the sensible thing to do, sir. The longer I talked, the cooler the water got." In hindsight I'm sure that he pondered on the 'what if' in a quiet moment afterwards.

Governor's report or adjudication was a means of fairly dealing with any rule infringement by prisoners. Enacted as a type of minor court situation, a fair hearing could be granted to both the reporting officer and the accused prisoner, who would be invited to plead guilty, or not guilty. The presiding Governor or his deputy decided to either dismiss the charge, or hand out a suitable punishment, which would depend upon the severity of the offence. There was a list of rule breaches, each having a number and could include: using threatening or abusive language towards an officer; possession of an unauthorised article; affray with another prisoner; refusing labour. The Governor ruling on all these lesser offences would give out suitable punishment. This might include a number of days in segregation or a loss of privileges, such as use of a radio or access to tobacco. A suspended award could be handed down to be added to any future awards, should the recalcitrant offender fail to see the error of his ways. More serious offences would be: staff assault; GBH to a fellow prisoner; arson or a group act of indiscipline, such as a riot or similar act that would cause danger to prison staff or property. In these cases a Board of Visiting Magistrates could be brought in to hold a court in the fullest sense and had the power to add a significant amount of time to a guilty prisoner's sentence.

In the days and sometimes weeks leading up to a major incident in a prison, the atmosphere is like that which precedes a thunderstorm, oppressive, uncomfortable and felt by staff and prisoners alike. So much so that it is often a relief when the storm breaks and the air is cleared. Towards the end of my first year at Gartee intelligence was being gathered, suggesting that the taking of a hostage or a major act of indiscipline was being planned and driven by the IRA contingent and their followers. Staff vigilance was ramped up to the highest level and informants on all four wings were quizzed as to the nature of any impending disruptive action. All insisted that they knew nothing and it was apparent that whatever group was responsible were either playing their cards very close to their chests, or were capable of threatening and frightening other prisoners into silence. At the start of the work day all prisoners would leave the main prison for labour in the workshops, via a manned vestibule adjacent to B wing and be counted whilst doing so. B wing was very significant to the following incident in that an additional segregation unit had been established on landing 3 that held prisoners under Rule 43. Any prisoner could request protection from other prisoners under this rule if they felt they were in danger, whilst located among the general population.

On this fine spring morning and after days of rapidly escalating tension, the duty vestibule officer realised that rather than going to work, a number of prisoners, some IRA among them, were bypassing him and entering B wing instead. This happened quite rapidly and before staff could begin to contain the problem, a number of IRA and known subversive and disruptive prisoners, had made their way up to the three's and taken over the unmanned area outside the segregation unit. They banged on the gated door and asked to be placed under protection, a ruse to gain entry to facilitate the taking of staff hostages. They'd then lock themselves and the staff into what would have been a secure situation from which to stage a very long standoff. On hearing the banging an officer opened the segregation unit door, but not the gate behind it. As he quickly realised the gravity of the situation he slammed shut the door and reached for the alarm bell. By then the segregation unit phone was already ringing to tell him and a further two officers to sit tight; they were now trapped until the situation could be resolved.

Some twelve prisoners having had their plan failed, now found themselves at an impasse. Staff quickly assembled in numbers on B wing ground floor and it is fair to say that due to the speed in which the situation developed, there was a feeling on both sides for a while of "What now?" Control of the incident was rapidly assumed by an Assistant Governor called McKay who went up onto the landing stairs below the twelve men, to try and persuade them to surrender. However, after almost an hour of abuse from the men he returned to the ground floor. He informed us that in thirty minutes time he would try again, but he believed that force would be necessary to remove the men from the landing.

By the time I retired in 2006 very sophisticated tactics and equipment were employed in resolving situations such as these, but in the 1970's it was frequently down to hand to hand grappling and brawling. As we waited for a decision to be made we all filed into the wing office. We removed our ties, keys and chain, wrist watches and emptied our pockets, keeping only our issue staves in the sleeve pocket of our trousers. Only a Governor grade could give permission for an officer to draw his stave, or 'stick' as it was known. Use of it without sanction, unless you felt your life was definitely threatened, was a disciplinary offence. The time waiting to be deployed to an incident such as this is always the worst. The adrenalin builds to the point where you are like a coiled spring and just want to get it over and done with.

After thirty minutes we were assembled at the bottom of the stairs in eight ranks of two; the stairs on the wings were not wide enough for three men to have sufficient arm room to operate in such a situation. The teams' biggest officers were naturally placed at the head of the group. I found myself in the second rank behind two huge officers, one of whom I think was called Barry who was a mountain of a man. With Assistant Governor McKay leading and us following quietly out of sight, we made our way up the stairs to see if or not a peaceful end could be brought to the situation. As usually happens during incidents like these, a leader and mouthpiece had come to the fore. On this occasion it came in the shape of one Harry Johnson. Known as 'Hate 'em all Harry' he did indeed hate staff and prisoners alike, along with all that swam, walked or crawled. He was connected to the London underworld and liked everyone to know it; he was loud, violent and a pain in the arse to all and sundry.

Before AG McKay had even opened his mouth to speak it was obvious that there would be no peaceful resolution to the standoff. Five fruitless minutes or so of him asking the group to surrender followed. Now with spittle on his suit from the prisoners above and whilst retaining his composure, he turned to our ranks and simply said "Take them down." As we surged up the stairs the keenest of the prisoner group led by Johnson came forward to meet us, then disaster. Big Barry misjudged the top step and stumbled forward as Johnson aimed a punch at him, barely connecting. Johnson then followed up with a vicious kick connecting solidly with the side of Barry's head. Barry did not seem to register the blow at all and as we passed him he was well on the way to having a roaring and swearing Johnson on the deck. The battle was over in minutes with no serious injuries to either side. The more serious combatants were placed in the segregation units and their less enthusiastic acolytes, back in their cells, pending Governors report. Or, in the case of Johnson, to be brought before the Board of Visiting Magistrates charged with an assault on a member of staff. What transpired at that hearing became part of prison lore.

Placed in front of the Magistrates and flanked by two officers, Johnson had the assault charge read to him and was asked if he pleaded guilty or not guilty, to which he replied proudly, "Oh, guilty." Big Barry was then asked to give his evidence and began as all prison statements do with the date, time and place of the incident, stating "I was at the forefront of a group, tasked by AG McKay with the removal of prisoners from number three landing, B wing," etc; so far so good. Then Barry went on to describe how he had stumbled on the top step and Johnson had kicked him in the head. On hearing this Johnson went berserk and began roaring "You're a liar, he's a fucking liar! I punched him in the face, he went down and then I kicked him in the head." Unable to silence or calm him down he was placed back in his cell whilst the Magistrates decided what sentence to pass. He had talked himself into extra prison time, but for him it was all about 'face' and reputation. He could still be heard bellowing from his cell, "He knows the fucking truth; I decked him fair and square."

Prisoner on prisoner assaults can be spontaneous and explosively violent. However, it tends to be the pre planned attacks that are the most injurious and nasty. Very often a 'chiv' or a pointed stabbing weapon fashioned from plastic, metal or wood will be used, usually with a crude edge which produces a deep and dirty wound. I came on duty one day into the aftermath of what had been in effect an attempted murder. Following photography of the victim's cell by the police and after due process, I was tasked with clearing the cell and arranging cleaning. It was obvious from the amount of blood involved that this had been a very serious attack and the injured prisoner was lucky to survive it. It was some months later that I read the victims account of the attack and chilling reading it made too. His assailant had fashioned a chiv from an eight inch length of thin mild steel stolen from a workshop, the improvised weapon was about 10 mm thick and 32 mm wide and he caught his victim lying on his bed. Without preamble he attempted to stab him in the throat upon which the victim tucked in his chin, which was all but severed in the attack. He then began to stab the man repeatedly in the ribs, cold-bloodedly pausing to straighten the blade, having bent the weapon upon his victim's sternum. By the time he left the cell his victim was unconscious and foaming through the ribs from a punctured lung, but clinging to life. There was no question of guilt as the officer who found the injured man had seen his attacker leave the cell and in any case, the weapon was left at the scene with the assailant's fingerprints all over it. Several years would be added to the attacker's already lengthy sentence; all that violence coming about over the ownership of a transistor radio.

Among the various characters I recall and certainly one of the creepiest was a weird little prisoner everybody called Willie; a lifer who had stabbed a complete stranger to death in an unprovoked attack. Young Willie was a very disturbed lad who would often stare right through you and snigger or giggle. He would rarely sleep in his bed, instead curling up on his cell floor where he never seemed to sleep properly and spent the night fidgeting and very often wetting himself. We decided that Willie would benefit from the company of a pet. At Gartree the men were allowed to keep budgies for company and several prisoners bred them successfully. So between the landing staff and one of the budgie breeders we fixed Willie up with a cage and a bird. This seemed to calm him somewhat and nobody was surprised when he asked for a second bird a couple of weeks later. The day after he was given the second budgie staff realised that the first one had vanished overnight. When asked about its whereabouts Willie announced that it had died and he had flushed it down the landing recess toilet. Both staff and prisoners found this a dubious explanation, but he was given the benefit of the doubt. However, all became clear some days later when an irate prisoner came to the landing office. He had just found dear little Willie firmly holding his second pet budgie and forcing a biro pen through its head, all the while with a smile and a look of absolute concentration on his face. It was the end of pet ownership for Willie.

I successfully completed my twelve months probation in the spring of 1976 after an enjoyable time on the wing run by Principal Officer Arthur Ravenhill. At this point PO Ravenhill was to become head of the security group at Gartree and he offered me a place on his team. This was totally unexpected and I jumped at the chance, knowing full well that after only one year's service I was lucky indeed to be offered such a position. The Security department was responsible for searching workshops and prisoners as well as organising prisoner transfers and other high security escorts. Another facet of the department's work was police/prison liaison and intelligence gathering from IRA and other high profile prisoners which was fed back to police headquarters at Charles Street in Leicester. From the moment I began working Security, I loved it, particularly searching duties which I could never get enough of, constantly being dumbfounded at the sheer ingenuity of prisoners and the daily challenge of staying one jump ahead of them. In the course of this work I came up against some incredible characters, though none more so than David Ralph Martin, an escapologist beyond compare.

Though only possessing a basic education Martin was highly intelligent, a genius at compromising electronic security systems and an accomplished locksmith. All these things made him a very dangerous individual. Martin was born in Paddington on the 25th February 1947. By the age of 16 years he had made his first court appearance for the theft of a motor vehicle, for which he received a fine.

Two years later he was sentenced to three months in a detention centre for assaulting a police officer outside a nightclub. Upon his release he quickly resumed his criminal activities and in July 1967 at the age of 20 years he was convicted of obtaining property by false pretences, three cases of larceny, two cases of store breaking and the theft of a motor car. Sentenced to Borstal Training, it was from there that he made his first escape from confinement, by springing a lock and scaling a boundary wall. It was some time before he was recaptured during which yet another crime spree earned him 21 months imprisonment. Having served this sentence

71

Martin teamed up with four accomplices and his criminality became far more sophisticated. By the time they were arrested in January 1973, over 900 items of stolen property were recovered from them, worth by today's standards almost £400,000. Placed on remand in HMP Brixton, Martin boasted "No prison will hold me."

David Martin

It was a statement of intent and on the 30th May along with members of the 'The Wembley Mob', a notorious gang of armed robbers, he was involved with an escape attempt which very nearly succeeded. The gang confronted a prison officer with what was a very convincing pistol - in fact made of soap blackened with boot polish – and took his keys from him. Having accessed the prison's 'sterile area' (an area where prisoners have no usual access) they hijacked the visiting dustbin lorry and attempted to ram the prison gate, but the vehicle became jammed there. Leaving the vehicle now, a vicious fight began between staff and prisoners which continued out onto Lytham Road. Seizing their opportunity, Martin and two others pulled out the driver from a passing car and sped away, injuring an officer who had jumped onto the car's bonnet in an attempt to smash the windscreen. After about a mile they abandoned the car and had the nerve to hail a taxi. However, by now they were being followed by a police helicopter and were swiftly cornered and arrested.

This marked the beginning of a nine year sentence for Martin and it was during this time that our paths crossed at Gartree. I remember him very clearly: a bisexual cross dresser with aquiline features, a feminine walk, long flowing blonde hair and a prolific wearer of moccasin slippers who could make a prison issue shirt look like a blouse. His journey to us was an eventful one. His first prison on this sentence was HMP Albany on the Isle of Wight, where he staged his first unsuccessful escape attempt before being transferred to HMP Parkhurst. Now dressed in prison grey with yellow stripes and patches to mark him out as an 'E man' or escaper, it was a reputation he would continue to garner throughout this sentence and beyond.

By this stage of his criminal development, Martin had become very skilled at taking apart locks, reassembling them, and had gained an intimate knowledge of the various types. He remains after all my 32 years of service, the only man I ever knew who appeared to be able to memorise a key pattern from a mere glance and then replicate it in whatever material he had to hand. He also understood and had taught himself how to bypass electronic security systems which made him a containment nightmare and a prisoner to be watched at all times.

The most difficult key to replicate in the whole prison estate is the 'doubles' key, which is used as a secondary lock for additional and total security of strategic gates. Difficult, yes, but at Parkhurst, Martin fashioned not only a doubles key, but also a pass key (door master or any access key). Along with a fellow prisoner, both of them in items of stolen officers' uniform, calmly walked through and out of the main prison. Having evaded detection in plain sight beneath various cameras, they were captured by a dog handler after starting to cut through the perimeter fence with a pair of bolt croppers.

So far so good; the escape had been foiled, but no one could locate the replica keys used in the attempt. Later this proved as no big surprise as Martin had put them in a cylindrical tube, along with a portion of hacksaw blade and slid them safely up his rectum. Along with his companion Martin was placed in solitary confinement. Overnight he extracted the tube and sawed through the hinges of his cell door. Then next morning he inched his door open, released his accomplice and opened the segregation unit gate, before being spotted by staff. Locked away once more, but this time it was without their keys.

Further evidence, if any were needed, of Martin's ingenuity came one evening when an officer on night duty noticed an echo on his personal radio, which became more pronounced whenever he passed Martin's cell. This was reported to the Orderly Officer and Martin was unlocked and his cell searched. It was discovered that he had rigged up an aerial to his transistor radio which he had re-tuned to pick up the frequency used by the staff radios. For David Martin everything was a tool or an escape aid.

After several months at Parkhurst the staff there must have breathed a sigh of relief when he was transferred to HMP Long Lartin in South Littleton, Worcester. A prison using the most sophisticated security systems available at the time, cell doors were not opened by key, but were locked and unlocked electronically from the jail's central control room. It did not take long before Martin was able to bypass a control panel and open his own and his companion's cell door without it registering in the control room. So as not to draw attention to himself, he had sawn through his neighbour's cell bars over a period of weeks. One night the pair crawled out through the gap and escaped from the wing, before once again being captured and put in isolation once more. Martin knew full well that his chances of escape were zero, but it was his way of showing his contempt of the penal system.

So, bless his cotton socks, he was transferred to us at Gartree. He seemed to settle and liked to be called 'Davina', but everyone knew it couldn't last and he was watched hawkishly by every member of staff. Sure enough within weeks his cell door showed signs of being tampered with. He was caught with several unauthorised items, just bits and pieces to anyone who knew nothing about him. We knew full well that he was a magpie and could put anything to good use, so he was placed in isolation, with staff having him under observation round the clock. Now seeing nothing untoward, he was placed in a standard cell in the segregation block next to a prisoner called Joyce, a violent armed robber serving life.

The short version of this story is that possibly using the rectum, saw and key conjuring trick, Martin and Joyce removed their lower cell window bars and escaped the segregation unit. They slipped through a space so small that even given their slight build, one would have thought it impossible. In the short time he had been with us, Martin had made both a pass key and a double key with which the men let themselves into a workshop where they attempted to fabricate a ladder. Having run out of time they were found by the fire officer the next morning, calmly drinking tea in the workshop office. Due to his repeated escape and subversive activities, Martin served much of his nine year sentence in solitary confinement.

Subsequently, upon Martin's release, his criminal activities took a violent turn. He raided a London gunsmith and stole a large quantity of handguns and ammunition, after which he was always armed with two weapons and would have no qualms about using them. A period of serious criminality ensued and knowing he was armed and dangerous, the police were searching for Martin in earnest. Following intelligence and a stakeout, two police officers attempted to arrest him entering a rented hotel room whilst he was dressed as a woman. From a handbag he produced a .38 revolver as the two officers grappled with him. Dropping that, quick as a flash, he produced an automatic from his waistband. He was challenged "Armed Police, Freeze!", but levelled the gun to fire upon them hitting an officer before the other officer shot him. The bullet shattered Martin's collar bone, but he continued to fight. As they held him down on the ground, he was screaming, "You fuckers can't do anything right. Come on, finish me. Give me another one."

Hospitalisation and due process followed. Whilst awaiting committal to Crown Court in HMP Brixton, Martin made several representations to be heard at Great Marlborough Street Court. Here he would at first be handcuffed to two officers in his cell. Unfortunately, as he appeared quiet and subdued during his court appearances, this was relaxed and each time he was placed in the same cell – oh dear. He arrived at court on Christmas Eve 1982 and quietly entered his cell for what was to be the 28th and final time. Around mid morning prison staff went to fetch him from his cell, but he had vanished and the door was closed.

Martin had somehow got out of his cell, shut the door behind him and climbed through a skylight onto the rooftops, from where he entered the London Palladium through a service door. Wandering out through the Palladium's foyer, he lost himself in the Christmas crowds. It would be January in the New Year before Martin was captured, whilst trying to escape through the tunnels of the London underground.

In the meantime a tragedy took place when police opened fire on a yellow mini, in Pembroke Road in the city, believing the driver to be Martin. Challenging him and thinking that the man was reaching for a weapon, they fired, hitting him with several rounds. As he fell sideways from the vehicle they realised that they had in fact shot the wrong man. His name was Steven Waldorf and he survived to receive substantial compensation. The horrendous accident was also to have serious implications with regard to police firearms protocol.

David Ralph Martin had played his final hand and was given a 25 year sentence which he began to serve at HMP Parkhurst. It is there, following a heated row with other prisoners that he committed suicide by hanging on the 13th March 1984. When I heard the news I was saddened, not for him, but for the talent he wasted and directed to evil means. There is no doubt that he could have become a rich man by selling his skills to lock and security firms and suppliers, but instead he remained a criminal through and through. My most vivid memory of him was when I unlocked him one day in the Gartree segregation unit. I said, "When are you going to screw your loaf and just do your bird. You're not going to spring yourself from here." Bold as brass he said, "I might, with a little inside help?" Not believing I'd just been propositioned, I replied "Just get your fucking dinner Martin." He minced off, grinning like a Cheshire cat, not at all disappointed and totally in character.

The summer of 1976 was a hot one. Apart from one precious week's holiday in Majorca and a few days here and there, I saw little of it. With higher temperatures came frayed tempers, for staff and 'cons' alike. The situation was made worse by the fact that about a mile and half away, just over the Grand Union Canal, was a glue works. The glue was made from animal hide and bones. In the heat the stink was bloody awful and carried by whatever faint breeze got up, right into the prison. It was a pleasure to smoke that summer.

Two prisoners from that summer remain vivid memories for me. One was Flight Lieutenant Alistair Steadman and the other, John Brook; two very dangerous men, but for very different reasons. Flt Lt Steadman had been a pilot, stationed at the RAF base on Anglesey, flying a Vulcan which was at that time, the backbone of Britain's nuclear deterrent. In 1975 he received a nine year sentence for attempting to sell strategic defence plans to the Russians. When questioned by the police he admitted that he had extensive knowledge of strategic war plans, targets in Eastern Europe and was versed in counter measures used to confuse enemy defences. He had been under surveillance for some time by the Special Branch and was seen making regular visits to the Soviet consulate in London's Kensington Palace Gardens. He arrived at Gartree during that midsummer and being an aircraft enthusiast I went to have a look at him, though not before telling myself to avoid asking him anything about the Vulcan. RAF to the bone, he almost marched into reception; it must have been a conscious effort on his part not to salute. We had a tennis court at Gartree which was never used and so had no net. Steadman had only been with us a few weeks, when he requested that a net be put up, so that he might play during exercise time. I can see him now marching out to the court with a prisoner in tow, wearing crisp white Fred Perry shorts and top, and a towel under his arm. I always wondered if he was at the controls of the Vulcan that flew over me that autumn morning at Newby Bridge.

John Brook by contrast was a cold blooded killer at the start of a life sentence. He had a prosthetic eye. That was the one with a certain humanity about it, the other was the eye of a great white shark. When you were in his presence you knew instinctively what you were dealing with, he was known as the 'Barns murderer.'

On 5th November 1972, Robert Patience returned home from The

Barns restaurant, to find John Brook and his accomplice Nicholas de Clare Johnson, holding his wife Muriel and daughter Beverley at gunpoint. The pair had entered the house believing that the safe there held a large quantity of cash. Brook demanded the keys to the safe. When Robert began to stall for time, Brook put a pillow over the gun he was carrying, to deaden the noise, and shot Muriel in cold blood. Brook then instructed Johnson to tie up Robert and his daughter Beverley. After he had done so, Brook walked over and shot Beverley in the back, before he turned his attention to Robert. Once again, using a cushion to muffle the sound of the shot, Brook put the gun to Robert's head and pulled the trigger. In what was nothing short of a miracle, the bullet skidded off Robert's skull, producing just enough gore to convince Brook that he had killed him. The pair left with the contents of the safe, a meagre £90 rather than the thousands they had expected. After Regaining consciousness, Robert was able to phone the police and the three victims were taken to hospital. Robert and Beverley survived, but three days later Muriel died from her wounds. A man hunt was on.

The abridged version of what transpired next is that the police arrested an armed robber, called George Ince, for the murder and robbery. Ince insisted he had an alibi, but absurdly for the police, he would not disclose what that alibi was. So, the case went to court and that is where it became interesting. It seems that the police had been somewhat creative in putting together their evidence. Ince was forced to spill the beans in order to save his skin. On the night in question he had been in the bed and the arms of none other than Dolly Kray. Yep, that's right, the wife of Charlie Kray...yes, those Kray's. Whoops! Dolly visited her husband Charlie in prison. Amazingly, Charlie was very understanding and told her to give evidence at the trial of Ince. As a consequence he received a not guilty verdict. So then, who was the murderer? The hunt went on.

Many miles away in the Lake District, John Brook was working as a kitchen porter in the Salutation Hotel in Ambleside and living in a flat on Main Road, Windermere. Working alongside Brook at the hotel was a petty crook, Peter Hanson. Brook boasted about

'The Barns' murders, as they had come to be known and shown Hanson the weapon. Arrested for theft and attempting to curry favour with the police, Hanson blew the whistle on Brook, who was subsequently arrested. The weapon found under his mattress in his flat, was a forensic match for that used on the evening in question and the case was closed. Johnson was also found and committed for trial, along with Brook. On 19th January, Johnson was given a ten year sentence for manslaughter; Brook received a life sentence.

I came into the security office one morning, that hot summer in July, and was told to pick up Brook from his place of work and to subject him to a very thorough personal and cell search. Intelligence gathered suggested that he was planning an escape and had begun to gather items to enable the attempt. Myself and a colleague picked him up, took him to his cell, initially subjecting him to a rub down search. I then began a search of his cell, whilst he was kept outside with my opposite number. I recall that he seemed to have changed personality overnight, from non communicative and hostile, he was now chatting about football, the weather and most things, barring the meaning of life (see what I did there?). As I worked my way through his cell I found pieces of wooden coat hanger which had clearly been fashioned into something of purpose, but what? Then, as I lifted a loose piece of floor covering, I found a hacksaw blade and began assembling all the various parts I had found into…a bow saw. Brilliant! From there the obvious place to look was his cell window bars. Sure enough, he had almost cut all the way through one bar and filled the gap with soap. I replaced everything as I had found it, told Brook that nothing had been found and we returned him to his place of work. Returning to the security department, I submitted a report detailing the findings of my search. I added that I had left all the unauthorised articles in situ, in order that the night staff could hopefully catch him at work and perhaps seize any additional items I may have missed, or that had been brought to his cell since.

In the early hours of the next day, he was caught red handed at work with his saw on his cell bars and placed in the segregation unit. It fell to me to place him on the Governor's report for possession of unauthorised articles and attempting to escape. As we stood in the adjudication, his lip curled as I gave my evidence, and he stared at me with a look of total malice. He pleaded guilty to the charge, earning himself a lengthy stay in isolation, with loss of privileges. Whilst there, he told anyone who would listen that he intended to kill me. I believe that he meant it too, but he was very quickly transferred out from us. It would be nearly two and half decades before our paths crossed again; the prison world is a small one.

From at first being unsure about the 'career' I was about to embark on, I found to my surprise that not only did I enjoy the work, but I also appeared to be reasonably good at it too. As the hot summer gave way to late autumn, my wife and I spent a well earned fortnight back home, in Cumbria. It was during this time that I realised how homesick I was and how much I missed the landscape. On returning back to Leicestershire, we discovered that Fay was pregnant with our first child. I began to wonder, given the long hours I was working, just how much of parenthood I would be able to be involved in. I decided to apply for a transfer to HMP Haverigg. This was denied, much to my disappointment, but in the New Year of 1977, fate took a hand when the post of Officer workshop Instructor was advertised there. Without really thinking it through, I applied.

I attended an interview at Stag Place, in London and was offered the post of handweaving instructor at Haverigg. It sounded really quaint, rustic and interesting; what was there not to like about that? PO Ravenhill urged me not to take the job, advising me in no uncertain terms that it was a 'dead end' posting and it would be in my best interests to remain at Gartree, where my promotion prospects were good. I wavered a little in the face of that advice, but accepted the job anyway. My reasoning being that if I was going to be a father, then I would have time to spend with my wife and child. With the exception of overtime outside workshop

80

hours, I would enjoy the benefits of a five day week. Our son John was born at Leicester Royal Infirmary, on 14th April. Shortly afterwards I took up my post at Haverigg, to be joined by my wife and son some weeks later on 20th May.

CHAPTER SIX

Toto I've a feeling we're not in Kansas anymore
Dorothy, wizard of Oz

As I explained in an earlier chapter, all prisons are categorised A, B, C and D. Therefore an officer on transfer, or initial posting, knows pretty much what to expect in terms of regime and security. When I walked through the gates of HMP Haverigg I was totally baffled by the place, both the layout of it and the way in which it functioned. The large farm and industrial area, with its various workshops, was enclosed by a fifteen foot high fence, as was the sports field and works department which was home to the prison's tradesmen and maintenance staff. In contrast, the prisoner accommodation which consisted of five rows of World War II airmen billets, education block, library, canteen, segregation unit and hospital/dispensary were all in one big open zone, with a gymnasium and football field at the southern end of the area. The prison's radio network was operated from the gatelodge. With the exception of the Senior Officer in charge of the gate and an officer attending the main gate for pedestrian and vehicle access, the gatelodge was afforded no physical protection at all. It absolutely astounded me.

In terms of the regime at Haverigg, the establishment appeared to operate entirely on the basis that prisoners knew and understood all the rules and did as they were told. A penal utopia for staff, but time would tell just how tenuous this status quo was. All prisoners were employed in various ways. The farm area was extensive and given over to vegetable crops and a large piggery that stunk to high heaven. There were two work parties: 'S' party carried out various types of work within the prison and 'Q' party tasked with grass cutting and estate work around the prison officers' quarters, on nearby Bankhead. In addition, there were several workshops in the industrial area: a tailor's shop making prisoners shirts, a laundry, a machine weaving shed, a mailbag hand sewing shop and two handweaving workshops.

One of the latter I was to work in, alongside a guy called Harry, who was in charge there. Prior to beginning work in the handweavers, I was given very little in the way of an induction programme. I realised full well, before many weeks had passed, that I had made an awful mistake in trading interesting and engaging work for geographical location. In short, I very swiftly became bored to tears.

The looms the men worked on were very like the ones you might see in old photographs from the Scottish crofts. Other prisoners called the handweavers shop 'The Monkey Shop' on account of the arms and legs actions used to operate the machines. Whilst some prisoners disliked the work, others loved it and as they were on piece work rate, they could make a good wage from it. The end product was material that was cut into floor cloths. The prisoners were all loom operators, with the exception of two cutting the cloths to size and packing them up and two others. They worked on a couple of winding frames, loading weft onto perns, which were then used in the loom shuttles. The tedium of duty in the workshop was such that I used to take a turn on the winding frames, or knock out a bit of material on a vacant loom to stop myself going mad with boredom.

As workshop instructors worked a five day week we were available for evening duties on overtime, or rest day call-ins at weekends. A welcome boost to our wages; however I cannot recall what my weekly wage was after over three decades but the overtime did come in handy at times. Moreover, for those who didn't wish to do extra hours, there were the 'overtime bandits' who would gladly work it on their behalf. An evening duty might be patrolling the perimeter fence, or the prisoner accommodation, staffing the segregation unit, or 'block' as it was known, or supervising the education unit classrooms. Finally locking up at 20.30hrs to perform a roll check, we left duty at 21.00hrs.

A weekend call-in was spent staffing the dining halls for prisoners' breakfast, lunch and dinner. It was an orderly affair where the men were to fill a table before anyone sat at the next one and all prisoners were required to return their dirty trays to the server, for washing by the kitchen orderlies. By the time I retired from the service I had a hard time convincing young staff that each table used to have a pineapple shaped glass vinegar bottle on it, but it did. However, the time would come when that luxury would be hastily and sensibly removed. Other weekend duties would include overseeing football matches, patrolling the billet areas and perhaps assisting the wing censor. All prisoners' mail was opened and censored in those days. Postal orders and cash were removed and the money signed for by the prisoner. It was then placed into his private cash account, from which he could buy goods for himself.

In the 1970's the prison bookie and the tobacco baron were the big wheels and strong arm tactics could be used to call in a bad debt. It was not until several years later, when drugs began to find their way into prisons, that violence associated with their illicit trade became extreme and endemic.

When I took up post at Haverigg, in 1977, I think that the prisoner population there stood at around 390. They consisted of repeat offenders of various types: brawlers, burglars, car thieves and some sex offenders. Inevitably for some who found themselves in prison for the first time, depending upon the individual, it could be an upsetting and frightening experience.

In the main, prisoners were allocated to us at Haverigg from HMP Strangeways (Manchester), HMP Walton (Liverpool) and HMP Durham. The latter was the source of local Cumbrian lads and a draft arrived by coach from one of these establishments most weeks. The Scousers thought the Mancs were divvies (idiots), the Mancs thought the Scousers were all gobshites and the Geordie lads thought that the Scousers and Mancs were both gobshites and idiots. However, the one thing that all three factions agreed upon was the fact that every Cumbrian prisoner had been convicted and jailed for having improper relations with sheep. In spite of this rivalry, Haverigg's population rubbed along at this stage with the most disputes centered on football.

In dispersal prisons, such as Gartree, most staff made it their business to get to know the prisoners on their wing. Where possible, through a carefully distanced but cordial working relationship, staff got to know who these men were, what made them tick and what brought them to prison. In the case of the well known celebrity offenders it would have been all over the press and media, but every man had his back story as an individual. To get to know them to some degree was to be able to work with them at close quarters on a daily basis, both when things were running smoothly and when they were decidedly not.

From the moment I began working in the handweaving shop, I interacted with the men in a fairly relaxed and informal way, just as I had at Gartree. Haverigg, it seems, was a very different kind of establishment. After a few months in post I was taken aside by a fellow officer and quietly advised that my approach in dealing with prisoners was causing concern. It was felt that my attitude to the prisoners was seen to be too informal and tongues were wagging. Clearly I would need to tread carefully.

Over the many years that followed, as I met staff from other prisons and interacted with those who had worked in various establishments on 'detached duty'. I came to realise that in terms of regime, there was not a single parallel example of Haverigg anywhere across the whole prison estate, both for staff and for prisoners. This was due to two factors, I think, firstly, its geographical location and secondly, as a result of peculiarities of management, prevailing since its opening in 1967. These led to an amalgam of rules and working practices based loosely on those in closed prisons, open prisons, young offender's establishments and Borstals. For instance, each Saturday morning an inspection was held on all the wings which addressed their attire and cleanliness of rooms. Other requirements included, prisoners being required to make up a military style bedpacks daily, shirts were to be neatly tucked in at all times and walking on grassed areas was forbidden.

At odds with all the various rules and regulations was the fact that at start and close of work, prisoners moved across the prison with little or no supervision. Should a man be required by a probation officer, for example, then he would be let out of the workshop to make his own way there.

At Gartree we had a very comfortable tea room where snacks were available and officers were detailed to provide tea breaks for colleagues who were doing long and boring stints in the prison's workshops. At Haverigg, the facility provided was a small room where one could purchase a cup of tea or coffee and a biscuit, spending 15 minutes over it in mid morning and mid afternoon.

On many occasions operational requirements, such as hospital escorts, would mean that lunch was taken so late that it could be as close as 2 hours to your evening meal. That meant that one had to choose which was to be your main meal. Although we workshop instructors were effectively on a five day week, if we were required to carry out evening duties, often working alongside the 'discipline staff' at weekends, we could also fall prey to unpredictable meal times. Rather cruelly during this time, staff at Haverigg were strictly forbidden to take either a flask or sandwiches to work with them; a situation I found hard to accept. The man in charge of Haverigg was Governor Cowper Johnson. He was a highly intelligent, though wildly eccentric gentleman, whose behaviour at times was rather odd. All things considered I felt that I had "Gone down the rabbit hole."

Having completed my first 12 months as a workshop instructor at Haverigg, I was summoned by the prison's industrial manager, to be given my annual report. I was not at all concerned; all my previous reports had been excellent. As far as I was aware, I had completed my year without causing, or experiencing, any problems at all. However, I was wrong.

CHAPTER SEVEN

I Try real hard to be Just Like I Am, But Everybody Wants You to be Just Like Them
Bob Dylan

I duly presented myself to the Industrial Manager - a civilian in charge of workshop staff and production - and his senior workshop instructor. In short order they informed me that whilst I had been posted into Haverigg with glowing reports and references, I had proven to be a disappointment to them: I was not fitting in well; showing little enthusiasm for the job; too informal in my dealings with prisoners and that I displayed a blasé approach to security. I was astonished. I railed inwardly at the latter accusation coming from a civilian manager, in a Category C establishment that couldn't decide if it was open or closed. I had served in the security department of a maximum security establishment, without putting a foot wrong.

Without making so much as a token attempt to defend myself and now completely demoralised, I departed the interview with the sure and certain conviction that my transfer to Haverigg had been a dreadful mistake. If I am honest, I suppose I did show very little enthusiasm for the manufacture of floor cloths. When I applied for the post, I did so with a view to getting myself and my family back to Cumbria, without carefully considering the type of work I would be doing. In that, I was the architect of my own misfortune.

Whilst the work was dull, I was able to pursue a great outdoor life during my time off. The fells were close at hand and there was some very good beach fishing, just minutes away. On the weekend

I would crew for a guy called Arthur Irwin, who had a converted harbour launch in which he took fishing parties out to sea. She was registered BW56 and was a sturdy vessel. However, she was built for use on the relatively sheltered waters of a harbour and because of this, it's fair to say, she would have pitched and rolled on a wet lawn. Whilst at sea and oblivious to any of the party who were feeling slightly queasy (or worse), Arthur would stand in the wheelhouse scanning the fish finder, all the while scoffing greasy belly pork sandwiches.

He also liked to give his fishing parties value for their money and would stay at sea till the last minute, usually returning to his mooring with just enough water to get in. "We'll give it a bit longer." he would say, "Nowt spoiling."

On one memorable occasion we were out at sea, just over the Haverigg bar and well after the tide had turned, when a strong easterly wind sprang up out of nowhere and the tide began to ebb rapidly. Making a run for the moorings, we ran aground two or three times, before we finally came to rest on a sandbank, just short of our mooring but were able to take off our party by dinghy.

This presented us with the problem of an unmoored boat. So, off we went to Arthur's garage for a chain, then to the village garage from where we scrounged an old car engine block. Heading back out onto the sands we spent an hour digging a hole, put the engine block in and chained BW56 to it. A fine adventure and much more exciting than making floor cloths.

CHAPTER EIGHT

Keep a Clean Nose, Watch the Plain Clothes

Bob Dylan

Knowing full well that our Industrial Manager had marked my card, I decided to try and keep my head down and attract as little attention as possible. However, a few months into my second Haverigg year, I blotted my copybook once again. The weft winding frames we used in the handweaving shop were ancient and one of them was completely unusable. So, it came as no surprise when I received a phone call from the Industrial Manager, telling me it was to be disposed of. Delighted at this news, I sent a prisoner off to the farm manager to borrow a sledge hammer, with which I vented my frustrations on the old winding machine. I smashed it to smithereens, with the prisoners cheering me on as I did so. I believe this spectacle provided some much needed entertainment for us all during what would have been yet another lacklustre day.

After lunch that day I received yet another phone call, from the Industrial Manager, asking where the winding frame was, to which I replied that "I've disposed of it." At this he sighed, "Well, it's not down at the works store where it should be, so get it down there from wherever it is and give me the paperwork to say that it's been done." "Well," I said, "that will be difficult because I have smashed it to bits and thrown it on the prison's scrap heap." He slammed the phone down on me, which even now I think was bloody rude of him. Five minutes later, he arrived at the workshop and demanded to know how smashed up the machine was. "Very." I replied. He stormed off without saying a word (again very rude), but then he didn't need to; both he and I were mentally writing my second annual report.

Whilst working in a lower category prison such as Haverigg it is easy to forget that some of the men you are locking up may well be on a path to committing far more serious offences further down the line. During my time in the handweaving shop my colleague and I had very few problems with regard to prisoner on prisoner violence. One incident remains firmly fixed in my mind though. For some men, their first custodial sentence is a traumatic and frightening experience. These are the lads who are least likely to reoffend. I had one such prisoner in our workshop. The big quiet, nervous young man was serving a short sentence for some petty crime,and not at all suited to prison life, making him a target for much bullying. It is difficult for staff to offer protection to a vulnerable man, without making the problem worse for him by him being labelled a 'grass'. To be able to keep an eye on him, I had him working on a loom just outside our office. We also had a very strange young prisoner in the workshop at that time. He was a weird looking guy, who had a habit of following me around asking questions about Ulverston and the local area, all the while carrying the large pair of scissors which each loom worker was issued with. He was a Lancashire lad who had been a problem from very early age. His interest in Ulverston stemmed from the fact that as a boy he had been put into Stone Cross, the special school there. He talked about the school and the town constantly and stated his intention to take up residence at the Kadampa Buddhist Temple. There was something very dark and intense about him; he was the least likely Buddhist I could imagine.

I was writing up prisoner's wages one morning, when I saw 'weird guy' advancing towards the vulnerable young lad outside my office, with his scissors held dagger fashion in his hand. I quickly jumped out of the office and put myself between the two men holding out my hand and making a 'gimme' gesture for 'weird guy' to hand over his scissors. The workshop began to quieten as prisoners stopped work to watch. The situation resembled the western saloon scene, when the piano falls silent and a tumbleweed blows through. For about 30 seconds the guy stood stock still, staring right through me, before finally surrendering the scissors with the most unsettling smile on his face; one I would describe as a mixture of malevolence and amusement. He was removed from the workshop and I placed him on the Governor's report for his actions. Following his adjudication he was transferred to another jail from where he would have been released as he'd come to us close to the end of his sentence.

At close of work that day, the young prisoner who was visibly shaken by the incident, came to me and thanked me profusely for intervening, insisting that 'weird guy' really was intent on stabbing him because he said I had been staring at him. I told him that the guy was an idiot who was just trying to frighten him and that he would not be seeing him again anyway. Two or three months later a prisoner came in to work and said to me, "Remember that weird dickhead with the scissors boss? Well, he's just murdered this old dear. Seems she caught him burgling her house and he topped her." Before I could reply he added with a smirk, "Wanna know the weirdest thing about it boss? He hacked her to death with a pair of her scissors. How mad is that? It was in our Mam's local paper. She brings it in for me." I think the frightened kid was right, 'weird guy' was going to stab him. Perhaps during that 30 seconds standoff he was weighing the odds. I will never know.

The late 1970's brought a change of Governor to the prison, but no change of regime. Haverigg plodded on in its own unique way. However, things were beginning to change throughout the prison estate in general and Haverigg was not to be an exception. As the 70's drew to a close, it was noticeable that prisoners were becoming more confrontational and staff were beginning to find small amounts of drugs fairly regularly.

By now I was working in the prison's tailor's shop where the men made the striped prison issue shirts; slightly more riveting than making floor cloths, but only marginally so. It was around this time that I discovered Olympic style weightlifting and loved it. The gym instructor was a highly qualified coach in the sport. Against all the odds, he helped me along tremendously in developing the very demanding technique required to carry out the squat snatch/ clean and jerk successfully. After always avoiding any sport at all I had discovered one that I liked.

In 1981 I transferred from the tailor's shop to the net shop, where camouflage nets were being assembled for an M.O.D. contract. It was in this year that our second child Joanne was born. I enjoyed the change of work, but had resolved to leave the workshops and return to discipline duties as soon as an opportunity arose. Haverigg was now entering a phase the likes of which it had never experienced throughout its 14 year service life. A very different type of prisoner began to come through the gates and drug finds were now on the increase. Forget tobacco, drugs were to be the new currency. With it came the attendant violence that always arrives tandem with drug dealing, as users incur debts that they can't pay.

I had found my own way of dealing with prisoners, carrot and stick for sure, but I always preferred to use a put down, threat or a good old fashioned rollicking as opposed to an adjudication and tiresome form filling. If this approach didn't work then you always had the rule book, but begin with the rule book and you were denied the flexibility I always preferred. My methods made me unpopular to work with. I was seen as a maverick, a loose cannon, but by and large I had the respect of prisoners and was not at all averse to laughing and joking with them, even at my own expense.

I got into an altercation in my workshop one day, with a little angry Mancunian prisoner who threatened to break my jaw. I let him have a good rant and then said to him calmly, but in a loud enough voice for the workshop to hear, "You know what you are kid?" "No," he replied, "what am I?" I said "You're a Capodimonte gangster!" Thinking that I had paid him a compliment of some kind and perhaps likened him to an Italian mobster, he looked up at me and snarled in my face, "Fucking remember it." upon which the whole workshop began laughing. He swaggered away quite satisfied that they were laughing at me, until someone told him that he had just been described as a tiny china figurine. A loss of face like that is worth more than any form filling and a good deal more satisfying.

In late 1981 I suffered a serious back injury which was to bring my weightlifting to an end. Whilst performing deadlift repetitions in training and with a considerable weight on the bar, I felt a thud in my lower back, followed by a searing pain which brought me to my knees. It would be almost a year of varying degrees of pain before I received a correct diagnosis. In spite of the fact that I had handled that kind of weight before and was wearing a support belt I had snapped off a lateral process, one of the lugs that project at right angles from the discs in the spine. An x-ray showed that it had in fact set itself. However, it caused me some discomfort for quite a while as a result of the damage that had been caused in that area, due to the fracture.

This was about the time when the country was going marathon crazy and several of the guys at work took up the sport. My friend Stuart Barnard, who had transferred from Gartree to Haverigg like myself, was training hard and suggested that I give it a try too. Now these fellas were like racing snakes, whilst I had built myself up to the proportions of a brick lavatory. Against my better judgement I decided to humour them and went out for a very breathless shamble around Haverigg's sea

Check out the tiny shorts and '80s moustache

94

wall, to see what all the fuss was about. It was the start of a decade of running which I enjoyed immensely, completing 9 marathons (best time 03.26), several half marathons and road races (best 10K time 35 mins 59 secs), numerous fell races and challenges culminating in my running from Shap to Ravenglass in 1988. That route took myself and a companion right across the Lake District, but sadly proved to be my swan song as far as long distance running was concerned. Subsequently, I was forever dogged with knee problems. Nevertheless, over the years I have continued to manage an occasional race and some light jogging, but it has been many kilos since I was fleeter of foot.

Crossing Black Combe summit during the fell race November 1983, and trying to catch Chris Brasher (I didn't)

CHAPTER NINE

A Change Would Do You Good
Sheryl Crow

In 1982 an opportunity presented itself for me to leave 'industries' to resume regular 'discipline duties' working on the wings and I grabbed the chance. At this time prisoners were still housed in the lines of old WWII airmen billets and staff worked them as three wings: A and B wing; E wing; C and D wing. I was drafted on to C and D wing, two lines of billets where duties were varied and could include a stint on 'fence gate'. This involved manually opening and closing the main gate for half your stint and the other half patrolling the internal perimeter fence, which I enjoyed after the years shut up in the workshops. Other routine duties were censors office work, patrolling the wing and supervising mealtimes in the prison's dining halls. These were the very same dining halls where the RAF lads had taken their meals over half a century before.

The working hours were longer, but the variety of tasks was very welcome. The situation at Haverigg was becoming increasingly challenging and interesting as the 1980's progressed. Drug finds were now quite common, including for the first time class A drugs, such as Heroin. Along with all this came the anticipated prisoner on prisoner violence, resulting from unpaid debts and as groups vied with each other for control of supply.

The Governorship of Haverigg had changed once again to be assumed by a gentleman called Ian Lockwood. As a forward thinker, he was swift to support his staff and would go on to become the Prison Service's North West Area Manager. At his instigation an operations group was established, fielding dedicated searching teams on a daily basis. Among the contraband, the teams were routinely discovering an increasing number of weapons, improvised from variously sourced pieces of metal; blades known as 'shanks' or chivs in prison slang. With no incidences of prisoners presenting with stab or slash injuries up to that time, we assumed that the main reason for possession of these weapons was protection and/or intimidation…we were whistling in the dark.

On a spring morning in 1985, a young prisoner, against all the rules, ran from the wings into the prisons 'Centre', which housed the Chiefs and the detail office. Clutching a towel to his neck as he was apprehended, he said in a choked and panicked voice "I need protection boss." The principal officer, who stopped him just inside the door, asked him what was wrong with his neck. He removed the towel to reveal a deep gash across his throat which our hospital officer later said resembled a letter box. The man was obviously in shock, refusing to say what had happened to him, until he had been stitched and located safely in the segregation unit. It seems that he had run up a drug debt which he couldn't pay. A gang cornered him in his room, held him down and beat him, before one of them sat on his chest, calmly and cold-bloodedly cutting his throat. The assailants obviously expected him to bleed out on the spot. Horrific though the wound was, none of us could believe that even with the gash gaping open, there was very little blood loss. How the blade missed a vein or artery remains a total mystery.

Away from work, my recreation time was filled by running and volunteering on an archaeological site, further up the coast at Eskmeals. A team from Edinburgh University, led by Clive Bonsall, was carrying out an excavation on a Mesolithic (mid Stone Age) site on the raised beach there. At the end of the last Ice Age, sea levels rose and fell as the climate changed. As a rule of thumb, the old shoreline from that period of fluctuation can be found around the first contour on an Ordnance Survey map. Over the course of their investigations, the team gathered over 30,000 small pieces of worked pebble flint tools called microliths, left by the hunter gatherer people who lived or camped seasonally there. I became friends with several of the team and over the next few years went on to work with them in Northumberland and the Inner Hebrides. Fascinating stuff and a great diversion from prison work.

When I set out to write this book I was determined, in so far as was possible, to stay clear of the usual prison book format and not allow it to become a litany of violence and weirdness. However, the 1970's and 1980's were a time of social flux which saw violence on the streets of our cities and unrest building in our prisons. In the case of Haverigg, this would culminate in an explosive and destructive loss of control. The years of 1986 and 1987 were difficult ones for us at Haverigg. Prisoners became more and more confrontational, larger quantities of drugs were being smuggled in and violence steadily increased.

Two members of staff would be on patrol on the double billet lines of A/B wing and C/D wing, with one staff member patrolling the single line of billets on E wing. Management's answer to the increasing problems at the time was to have staff patrol on their own, in order to maximise cover and observation. As the situation deteriorated, we often ignored this directive and felt safer in pairs. To patrol Haverigg was like patrolling an unruly town. It was more akin to policing than the work carried out by our colleagues on the landings, in closed prisons, with cellular accommodation. Prior to showers being installed in the billet blocks, the original WWII bath houses and showers, which were situated between the rows of accommodation, were used as ablution blocks by the prisoners. The bath house blocks were an area where grudges were often settled and prisoners were very reluctant to take a bath, due to the vulnerable position this placed them in. For this reason, baths were removed by 1990 and showers installed, being much safer and more hygienic.

Evening duties during the dark winter nights were becoming increasingly fraught, with prisoners pushing fire and general alarms to run staff ragged. One winter's night in 1987, during evening association, there was a systematic extinguishing of outside lights by prisoners, either by switching them off manually, or simply smashing them. In the midst of this, staff were called to respond to an incident in the A/B bath house. What we found there was a semiconscious prisoner lying naked beside a bath tub, covered in blood and with severe injuries, both to his head and his body. On the floor around him were pieces of sweeping brush shaft which his assailants had broken over his body whilst beating him with them. The shafts had not snapped cleanly, but to a sharp point and had been used bayonet fashion upon him, causing several stab wounds.

With the lad drifting in and out of consciousness, an ambulance was very swiftly on the scene. When it arrived and medics began to remove the casualty, a number of prisoners gathered and began to hurl stones and other missiles at the vehicle while staff tried desperately to disperse them. My reader might well ask where they got the stones from. The fact is that the edges of the grassed areas in the jail were littered with them, but hey, the regime at Haverigg had been perfectly stable for 20 years, so why worry about a few rocks lying around. The rest of that evening shift was spent trying to get prisoners to return to their rooms for roll check. After some considerable time we were able to do so, but

In August 1986 I took leave and backpacked out to the French Alps for a solo trekking trip. Here I am in Chamonix, no shower and no comb, believe it or not I could just about tame that hair under my uniform cap but was constantly getting grief about it from my superiors.

more than one of us said that night "One of these times, they just aint gonna go behind their doors and then the excrement is going to hit the air extractor."

Stones were not the only potential weapon available to prisoners. On each of the tables in the dining halls were salt and pepper pots and those heavy glass vinegar bottles shaped like a pineapple which I mentioned earlier. From the moment I clapped eyes on them I realised their potential and nicknamed them 'vinegrenades'. During a power cut one evening before the emergency lighting kicked in, that's just what they became. As the lights went out, staff ducked behind tables while a hail of 'vinegrenades' burst around them with some wag shouting "Incoming!" These items were very sensibly withdrawn after the incident, but not before I was personally almost on the receiving end of one.

A good working relationship between officers and prisoners is essential for the smooth running of a wing, or workshop. This can be achieved through mutual respect, or simply by a member of staff and a prisoner, or prisoners, getting along very well. However, should a prisoner, or prisoners, take an extreme dislike to a member of staff, this always causes problems for themselves, the member of staff and the smooth running of the wing generally. Such was the situation I found myself in with a young Mancunian prisoner of mixed race, who for some reason no one could fathom, hated my guts from day one. He would try and cause an argument just about every time he came to the wing office. From information gathered through informants, it became clear that he was a bully extorting tobacco and other items, including drugs, from the more vulnerable lads. A man such as this disrupts the day to day duties of staff, but can also be an irritant to other prisoners who might be glad to see the back of him, should he fall foul of prison rules and be transferred. Even more so if they are in debt to him, or are scared of him, hence he was informed upon. When staff searched his room he was found to have an unfeasible amount of tobacco in his possession, along with several prohibited items, earning him a stay of several days in the segregation unit, following a Governors report and pending a transfer back to Strangeways.

On his second night in the Segregarion Unit, I was on evening duty, in charge with a junior officer. All meals were sent to the 'seg unit' from the main kitchen and a hotplate was in place down there from which to serve them. I knew full well that this guy was going to give me grief. Consequently, I told my opposite number to unlock him last for his tea, after we had fed all the other prisoners. I prepared myself for the expected verbal confrontation. The meal that evening was chips, eggs and baked beans, a firm favourite with all the lads but, when my Mancunian chum saw what was on offer he announced that he was "not eating that shit." Trying to lighten the moment I said "Come on kid, you know you want to. It's chef's special, everybody's favourite." In reply he shouted, "You fucking have it then." and threw the remaining tray of baked beans over me. Then he grabbed the 'vinegrenade' and launched it at my head. Fortunately, I had anticipated more air traffic and was able to duck out of the way as it shattered against the wired safety glass behind me leaving a star shaped crack there. He stormed back to be locked up, shouting to the other prisoners ``He called me a black bastard. He tried to hit me, so I fucking trayed the dickhead." Upon locking him back up, my colleague rushed down to check I was okay and found me covered in beans and announced with a straight face, "You're going to need a lot of toast with that Nico." Prison humour. I went off home to get a clean shirt and trousers, but word travels fast and before I had even left the jail, I had been the butt of every bean joke anyone could come up with.

Following this incident I used to entertain new staff by telling them the story. Standing behind the wired glass panel, I'd demonstrate how the damage to the glass corresponded exactly with the centre of my forehead. If you are in the prison service long enough you will turn almost anything into a laughing matter. It is how you navigate that environment on a daily basis and it lessens the stress for everyone.

A serious footnote to this story is that the day this guy was transferred, two different prisoners told me that he intended to "come back for me" when he was released and that he knew where

I lived (which was very likely as a prisoner on an outside grass cutting party would know where a number of the staff lived and could have told him). His stated intention was to slash me up in front of my wife and kids.

He had a lot of previous charges for this type of assault and I took the threat seriously; he was a violent offender who exercised little restraint.

I need not have worried, only two months after his release from prison he finally pushed his luck too far. In the middle of an argument, outside a Manchester nightclub, he was stabbed by a guy and died on the spot from his injuries. You live by the sword, you die by the sword.

CHAPTER TEN

I Predict a Riot

The Kaiser Chiefs

Following cease work and completion of the evening meal on Friday, 3rd June, 1988, it was clear that a faction amongst the prisoners were becoming increasingly restless. Several acts of vandalism were being carried out around the establishment. Windows were being broken, waste bins set alight and damage being caused to plumbing in parts of the prisoner accommodation. The prison was a tinderbox, only requiring a spark to ignite it. This spark was provided when prisoners were ordered to remove all pictures and posters from the external walls of their rooms.

By Saturday, 4th June, the sabotage and vandalism perpetrated by the inmates had reached a whole new level. With such a large percentage of toilet facilities being destroyed and in order to keep the establishment in a sanitary state, emergency plastic 'chamber pots' were being considered for issue. It was with a huge sigh of relief that we managed to lock down the jail that night. However, the auxiliary night staff were run ragged till almost dawn next day, answering false fire and emergency alarm bells.

All of Sunday, 5th June, was tense and stressful. A large proportion of the prisoners were reticent and the rest were becoming increasingly bullish, challenging and disruptive. I was scheduled for evening duty that night and returned to my quarter, in Bankhead, for my tea at 16.00 hrs. As I came out to return to work, a fellow officer, Roger Singleton, pulled up in his car and gave me a lift. Also in the car was Officer Brian Morris; a smashing bloke possessed of a great sense of humour and a pleasure to work with. It would be the last time I would see Brian alive.

As per routine, we served the prisoners their evening meal. The process was completed with little in the way of problems and all staff left the dining halls to take up their respective duties for their evening shift. I was to spend the first half of mine supervising the A and B lines TV room, grateful for a chance to sit quietly after the stress of the previous two days.

By around 18.30 hrs the TV room had emptied, leaving only myself and two nervous looking lifers watching some soap opera. I was just about worn out and there had been no radio traffic, so it did not register with me that something was very wrong. That is until the door burst open. An officer rushed in shouting "Fucking hell Nico, they've been trying to contact you. The place has gone up; they are rioting on C and D lines." During this time it was not uncommon to be issued with flat, or near flat radio batteries. Upon checking I did indeed find my radio to be dead.

After turfing the two reluctant lifers out of the room, I locked up and ran to The Centre to get a fresh battery and a spare. It was obvious that I was going to need them. When I arrived there I found the Orderly Officer, Neil Houston and his Assist Senior Officer, Ted Tosh, grimly waiting for an ambulance. Brian Morris was dead at their feet. He had suffered a massive heart attack and all their attempts at CPR (Cardiopulmonary Resuscitation) had failed. I have always been ashamed that the chaos that ensued was such that I did not feel the full impact of Brian's passing until the next day.

The flashpoint for the riot was when Officer Mick Purvis caught a prisoner smashing windows with a broom shaft on C and D lines. When ordered to stop, they set about Mick with said broom shaft. Whilst defending himself and being distracted, he was set upon by a group of inmates who threw a jacket over him, with the clear intention of both taking him hostage and giving him a beating. However, Mick was having none of it, fighting his way free and escaping. During the subsequent inquiry he was told that he would receive an award for his bravery; he watches the post to this very day in the hope that it may yet arrive.

When I arrived on C and D wing, staff were desperately trying to de-escalate a rapidly worsening situation. It was obviously hopeless. Prisoners increasingly began to feed off each other's excitement and aggression, fast becoming an almost single entity; one which had the clear intention to cause as much mayhem and destruction as possible.

At around 19.00 hrs the first prisoners smashed through and climbed onto the roof of D7, precipitating similar acts all across C and D wing. The mood was now becoming increasingly ugly. Fearing for the security and integrity of the perimeter fence, an order came from the management (who were totally divorced from the situation whilst in the gatelodge and radio room) for staff on the scene to spread out, secure and guard the fence to the rear of the rioting wings.

By now A and B wing were joining the party and that order was madness. I told the staff who were with me that we should disregard it and instead make a run for the gate area using whatever cover we could. The escalating situation meant that within minutes we would find ourselves trapped at the far south west reaches of the prison, most likely be taken hostage or worse. So that is what we did, just managing to keep ahead of a mob that was at our heels the whole way.

Everything possible was against us that night. Of the 515 inmates housed in the jail, we had no idea how many would become actively involved in the riot. Also, due to the prison's geographical location, it would be several hours before staff from other prisons could come to our assistance. Haverigg staff in the main responded magnificently, rapidly reporting for duty as soon as the word was put out. Cumbria Constabulary pulled out all the stops to provide as many backup units as they could. This was to prove invaluable as the largest prison escape in Britain, for over half a century, was about to take place.

Tuesday, June 7, 1988

RIOT

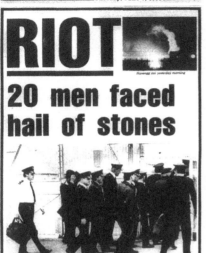

● Haverigg riot yesterday morning

20 men faced hail of stones

● THE thin blue line warders at Haverigg yesterday

By BILL MYERS

A THIN blue line of only 20 prison warders faced the terror of a full-scale prison riot at Haverigg, it was revealed yesterday.

At one stage as the highly charged atmosphere changed from frustration to fury, warders came under a barrage of stones.

Officers had expected some form of protest hours before the rioting.

A dramatic, last-minute plea for calm by the prisoners' new governor may have prevented even greater damage than the wrecking of 28 buildings and the escape of 25 men.

Details of the riots have been released by the governor Mr Ian Lockwood, who moved to the prison less than six months ago.

Mr Lockwood's day began with tragedy. He had been on leave and returned to the prison on Sunday after one of his officers, Brian Morris, died on duty, apparently from a heart attack.

There is no connection between the warder's death and the ensuing riot.

Trouble began around 7.30 p.m. apparently over the prisoners being denied pin-up posters in their rooms. A heater was wheeled to order men to their dormitories as normal. The riot began in C wing.

● Turn to page 3

Est. 1898   Monday, June 6, 1988

RIOT

● 26 prisoners flee Haverigg
● 13 recaptured this morning
● Arrests at Newby Bridge
● Evacuation of nearby families

Huge fire seen from two miles

Prison blazes after row over cell pin-ups

● HAVERIGG prison last night: police held firemen back for 10 hours as blaze raged

By BILL MYERS, MIKE RUSHTON AND ALASDAIR NORTHROP

AN INTENSIVE search throughout Cumbria was under way today for 13 escaped prisoners after a night of riots and fires at Haverigg jail near Millom.

Twenty-six escaped from the low security jail—which holds 44 prisoners serving life sentences — as 100 inmates went on the rampage. Half were recaptured by first light.

Plumes of smoke were visible ten miles away at dawn. A huge fire raged out of control.

Police ordered firemen to stay out of the prison and they were only allowed in put out the first ten hours after the riot had begun.

Motorists

Witnesses saw a small group of prisoners chased and captured by police in Millom town centre.

Another is believed to have been caught at Foxfield, near Broughton.

A road block has been set up at Dunnet Bridge on the main road out of Millom.

Queues of up to a dozen Vickers-bound cars were held up this morning as police questioned motorists.

A lone police officer told drivers: "There are some prisoners out from Haverigg, have you seen anything?"

Road blocks were in force all night on the approaches to the prison while police were still unsure how many had escaped.

Bystanders and Press men on the main prison outing road were moved on by of

● Turn to Page 10

A mortgage from the F

Furness
BUILDING SOCIETY

and y

saf

Men seen at Corney — and Windermere

● From Page 1

● BACK into the fray: police in riot gear return to the prison after a break

She looked out of her window at midnight and saw three men in prison uniform wandering up her street ... 'I was really terrified ...' she didn't know if they had been caught

BONFIRE

HELICOPTER

I was really terrified, she said.

● POLICE threw a cordon around the prison

● EVACUEES 'We are frightened,' said a warder's wife

HAVERIGG HANGOVER

quiet on the western front: a hard day's night for officers.

A break from the riot

rison records rescued as the balloon went up: TV rooms, library, gym, half the jail wrecked

COST of the ning violence destruction in Haverigg Jail being counted after prisoners been moved to jails.

any as 28 buildings ut to the torch ands of pounds of glass is being ed

tal of 25 are now to have escaped h two main holes the 17 ft perimeter The holes have now epaired

Governor Lockwood

The greatest vandalism was to those parts of the prison most used and enjoyed by prisoners

Television rooms, the library, the gymnasium

and dozens of the men's own rooms were wrecked

The governor is making an inquiry into how much of the prison is still usable

Windows, washbasins toilets, asbestos roofs and recreation equipment were broken

Quick thinking prison officers saved all the jail records on inmates and staff, said the governor, Ian Lockwood.

He said prisoners lived, usually one to a room, in billets 'They have got quite flimsy doors

'The doors are closed on them at night and they are expected to stay inside.'

Twenty officers had been guarding C-wing living quarters and recreation area where prisoners were enjoying Sunday evening television and games

This was the normal number

HURT

There had been no tension at the prison and officers did not need to make a physical end to the riot

'When the prisoners were surrounded and secured the activity just died down,' he said

Only one prisoner was badly hurt in the rioting He surrendered himself to officers

Emergency meeting of Millom Town Council

AN extraordinary meeting of Millom Town Council last night questioned police and prison officials

Councillors were concerned there was no public warning of the escapes and that prisoners had breached the fence.

Millom clerk Mrs Olive Townsley said

'The prison spokesman said a public warning might create unnecessary panic. Assurances were given that the category of prisoners was suitable for a prison like Haverigg.'

Police Supt Chris Heslop and Insp Ray Cole were at the meeting and raised the

possibility of giving the public warning of a breakout through neighbourhood watch schemes.

Mrs Townsley said: 'Councillors have raised this point about a warning before and the reply that is always given is that it would create a panic, so we have to accept that.'

Ve expected something like this

BILL MYERS

E had been warn f a Haverigg style in for six years, said Elliot, national ex spokesman for the n Officers' iation

Haverigg officers and those drafted in have coped magnificently but were unhappy at what had happened

'There was absolute devastation in there,' he said

Much of the blame for

violent prison disorder nationally was due to re categorisation, where prisoners with serious crime convictions were sent to lower security prisons

Re-categorisation was going on at an alarming

rate without the prison staffing to cope with it

'There was absolute sheer violence in there

'It might have taken the local staff by surprise but nationally we have been warning against this for five or six years,' he said

How the local North West Evening Mail reported on the riots.

From the author's scrapbook

False alarms as three remain at large

Inspector Neill r, in charge of the operation at Millom aree men were still loose and the public een ringing in with ngs this morning. re very interested in

the co-operation of the public and this morning we have had indications that there might be a convict still in the area.

'We have had false alarms such as people going to work and about

their lawful business but every one is worth checking out.

He said the vast majority of escapees were rounded-up quickly after the breakout and many did not get far past the

perimeter fence.

'We have looked at the possibility of people trying to escape from here and because of this we managed to get men in quickly

'Some gave themselves up at the fence.'

107

By the time we reached the gate area and made contact with other staff, parts of the jail were already alight. It was agreed that the gatelodge with its keys and main radio set should be protected at all costs. As the rioters advanced upon it, some seven or eight of us formed a line between two buildings to hold them off, providing a temporary choke point. They could actually have easily outflanked us. Fortunately, they were so intent on attacking our small group, they failed to appreciate or exploit this option.

As we held the line against twenty to thirty rioters, we did so with no personal protective equipment whatsoever. In fact a couple of staff were using dustbin lids as shields, whilst doing their best to avoid the missiles that were coming our way. The first offerings were stones and sundry items of debris, followed by pieces of broken glass skimmed at us like frisbees. They were the most frightening of all because it was difficult to see them coming. Then things took a really bizarre turn. We came under attack from a hail of tinned pilchards, ammunition plundered from the victualling store. The bombardment was all one way until a young Irish officer called Davey Holden shouted "Throw it back at the bastards!" So we began to make it two way traffic, much to the consternation of our assailants, some of whom began laughing as if it was a great game. However, the situation was becoming increasingly violent by the minute. Word was coming via the radio net that large numbers of prisoners were attempting to breach the fence.

As more Haverigg staff began to arrive to back us up, we were allowed to fall back and phone our families to alert them to the danger of a mass breakout. With the disturbance escalating and until the situation was brought under control, a plan was put in place which facilitated their evacuation to the Magistrate's Court buildings in Millom.

Bored with the standoff at the gate area and realising that the real party was taking place in the main prison, the rioters began to back off and join the increasing numbers who were looting, setting light to buildings, settling old scores and generally unleashing hell. At Haverigg there were no contingency plans for an event such as this, because it was never envisaged that such a calamity as this could ever occur. It never had before, right? All this coupled with the fact that more than one member of middle management had little, or no experience, beyond that of a category D regime. Some had been at Haverigg for most, or all of their service, leading to an almost decisional paralysis when the inmates went totally off script.

As I have stated previously, Haverigg with its sprawling layout and non cellular accommodation was more like an unruly housing estate/town than a prison. Here we were fighting with prisoners street fashion and they proved very good at it indeed. Many of these guys were veterans of the Toxteth, Croxteth and Moss Side riots of 1981. We were up against 'pros', not just cons.

On the eastern reaches of the jail, the prison Hospital and the Segregation Unit were sited. Locked in the seg unit a member of staff was trapped and waiting (hoping) for the arrival of the cavalry. Clearly a rescue had to be undertaken, but the prison grounds were becoming increasingly and violently unnavigable. It was decided to cut through the perimeter fence into the adjacent works compound. From there we could extract both the officer and the hospital orderly. The latter would have been deemed a grass, a staff lackey and subjected to a severe beating. The operation was a success. Upon arrival back at our muster point, the gallant works staff that had helped pull it off, had brought with them a bundle of pick axe and hammer shafts from the store. We used these to arm ourselves; our light, short personal staves being useless in the circumstances.

The paucity of riot equipment at Haverigg that night is best summed up thus: as we prepared to make a short tentative advance into the prison, we were each given the choice of one item of protection. We could have one of the few long staves available, a helmet, a shield or a hammer/pickaxe shaft. Well they say if you're going to have one, then have a 'biggun' and so for sheer deterrence value, if nothing else I opted for a pickaxe handle. Instantly becoming my new best friend, it stayed loyally by my side as we danced the quickstep till dawn.

As the night progressed staff numbers began to swell. Fully equipped units from the Lancashire prisons began to arrive, along with their dog handlers. This meant that we could fall back from any ground we had gained to take up other duties. Meanwhile, a comprehensive advance into the main prison could begin to take the surrender of any inmates not involved in the disturbance, locating them in a place of safety, whilst also, whenever possible, arresting groups or individuals who were still active and hostile. The large machine weaving shed and the equally large and adjoining tailors workshop in the industrial area were allocated for the holding of none hostiles. This area with its high fences had not been breached. In each of the repurposed workshops, three members of staff were on post to patrol and supervise the surrendered prisoners, whose numbers began to swell rapidly during the early hours of Monday, 6th June. I was in charge of the tailors holding area, along with my two staff. By the time 04.00 hrs came around, ourselves and the adjoining workshop, were containing 200 /250 prisoners, between six of us.

It was a tense few hours. We knew full well that a good number of the professed 'surrendered' had been actively involved in the riot. They had given themselves up, having had their fun and were now gathering in sufficient numbers to begin to cause havoc in the industrial area, or perhaps even to take hostages - a worry that is ever present during a loss of control in any prison.

Somewhere between 06.00 hrs and 07.00 hrs we six were relieved of our duties (very relieved actually) and instructed to report to the administration buildings in the gate area. A scene of frantic activity ensued throughout the night, as staff stripped the buildings of all prisoner and other records, placing them in safe keeping outside the establishment. For the record, the place of safekeeping was the horsebox owned by our Administration Officer, Barry Allen. This was then driven to his house where the vehicle and contents would remain under guard until the jail achieved stability once again.

Upon arrival at our muster point we were kitted out in full riot gear which had arrived during the night and were briefed. Whilst an accurate roll call was not possible, it was clear that a certain number of prisoners were still at large in the prison. We were to carry out a building by building search, the aim being to apprehend these last die-hards and any who might be in hiding, afraid to give themselves up. The prison hospital and dispensary had been looted and burned out. There were bloodied and used needles everywhere. We were instructed to search the burnt out billets whenever possible and we did not need to be told why. We all felt that someone must have overdosed; perhaps dying in the fires and so we steeled ourselves for what we might find.

As we carried out our sweep of the jail we established that in fact no one had perished as a result of the disturbance. Following

Author in burned-out prison canteen

some very brief hand to hand fighting, we were able to take into our custody all remaining hostiles before we were stood down at around 08.00 hrs. The prison was now flooded with support staff from other establishments; coaches and vans were already arriving to transfer prisoners to other jails far and wide, as space would allow.

Personal memories of the night
plus some facts and figures

1.   From Hansard House of Commons sitting 7th June, 1988, it was stated that the number of staff on duty at the time the riot began was 20. I cannot dispute this figure, but would add that the usual compliment for evening duty was lower than this. If there were in fact 20 of us, then it is possible that given the growing unrest that weekend, extra staff may have been deployed. After over 33 years, I have no clear recollection.

2.   In total, some 34 prisoners escaped from Haverigg that night, scattering to all points of the compass, some on foot and some in stolen vehicles. However, all but 3 of them were fairly swiftly recaptured though. As previously stated, this was the largest prison escape in Britain, for over half a century.

3.   In total some 28 buildings were destroyed by fire, resulting in 300 prisoner accommodation places lost.

4.   Hansard House of Commons sitting 7th June, 1988: It was asked by Dr John Cunningham (Copeland), whether it was the case that on the night of 5th and 6th June, there were only two qualified prison staff on duty, supported by seven Auxiliary Officers. Clearly, there were 20 trained and qualified staff on duty at the time the disturbance began. What Dr Cunningham was quoting were the accurate Officer staffing levels for the night shift.

5.   Hansard House of Commons sitting 7th June 1988: The Under Secretary of State for the Home Department, Mr Douglas Hogg, stated that at 19.30 hrs on the evening of 5th June, some 40 prisoners began causing damage to buildings. Additionally, it was not until 23.00 hrs that there was an escalation and staff had to withdraw.(Sorry Dougie old chap, that's not how I remember it. In fairness, your extreme honourableness you really needed to be there on the night)

6.   Such was the chaos that night, the only sustenance provided for staff were two urns of tea, which for the record

the next morning, remained half full and cold. Staff were instead drinking tap water throughout the night, whenever the opportunity arose. During our final advance into the prison, we came across several toffee bars around the looted prisoners' canteen, picking them up for a much needed sugar hit. Many of us had been on duty since 07.00 hrs the previous day and had not eaten for over ten hours. The Principal Officer leading our group ordered us to put them down at once, adding that our behaviour amounted to us being little better than the rioters. We were in no mood for this and our terse replies ensured that the order was ignored and not repeated.

7.   Having finally stood down from duty at around 09.00 hrs that morning, I barely remember throwing myself into bed, falling asleep in seconds having been on duty for 26 hours. My sleep was ruined about ten minutes later. A light aircraft and helicopter began orbiting the smouldering prison, taking photographs for the daily papers. In times such as these there is only one course of action. Tried and trusted, and so determined not to be denied my sleep, I retrieved a bottle of whiskey from our kitchen, got good and drunk and passed out on the settee.

8.   In the wake of the riot my previous Governor, Mr Gordon Lakes, who was Governor of HMP Gartree during my time there and now the Deputy Director General of the Prison Service was tasked with carrying out a full enquiry into the riot and its root causes. An extremely fair man, he interviewed every member of Haverigg staff and after exhaustive investigations published his findings. He concluded that security measures at the jail were inadequate by Category C standards, making several recommendations with regard to the regime, if memory serves me correctly. Nevertheless, I do recall clearly a nutshell statement from the report, published in our local paper, which blamed "long term lack of leadership and managerial neglect" for many of our problems.

To be fair to our reasonably newly arrived Governor, Ian Lockwood, I feel and always have, that he received a 'poisoned chalice' in his posting to Haverigg. The regime and infrastructure not being fit for purpose, due to the type of inmate we were housing by the time he came to us. Further questions were raised in The Commons as to whether there had been 'cosmetic recategorisation' of serious offenders, in order to send them to lower category jails where much needed prisoner places existed. Also at the time, George Elliot, the National Executive spokesman for the Prison Officers Association, stated that he in fact believed this to be the case.

During the official investigation, staff from the prisoner allocation units of HMP Walton and HMP Strangeways were brought to Haverigg and given a tour of the establishment. To their credit, they left shame faced and embarrassed. In their total ignorance they had been sending completely the wrong sort of prisoner to us, in the mistaken belief that we had cellular accommodation. When they saw the burned out WWII Airmens' billets, their mouths fell open. Our geographical location and status as Cumbria's remote and only prison, far removed from any others, had sealed our fate. We were the jail that common sense forgot, toddling towards disaster with our own peculiar and unique regime, frozen in time since 1967.

In the wake of the riot the future of HMP Haverigg hung in the balance. It was due in no small part to the efforts of Governor Lockwood that the prison was granted a future. This was a relief to those of us who were not keen to be posted elsewhere and was welcomed by the local community, given its contribution to the town's employment and overall economy. The main problem facing management was how to increase the jail's population to a realistic level, having lost some 300 accommodation places. A certain amount of refurbishment was possible, though several of the damaged billets had to be demolished. It was decided that the best solution, in the short term, was to house prisoners in shipping container style accommodation. It proved to be quite adequate and not unpopular with the prisoners who christened them 'spam cans'. As our staff offices had been burned out, we relocated to portacabins, which we found comfortable and served us perfectly as a temporary measure.

As the enquiry recommendations began to be implemented, areas of the prison were 'zoned off' with 15 foot high fences. These would enable staff to lockdown individual areas in the event of a disturbance, to prevent the problem spreading and to allow them to deal with any given situation swiftly. Given the shortcomings of billet accommodation, many of us were dismayed to learn that the plan was to replace the old airmens' billets, which had been demolished, with new billet style units , though they would have lockable doors on all rooms, which was some compensation.

Later that summer, we experienced yet another disturbance at Haverigg. This time, a smaller and relatively brief event, which was swiftly quashed. We had learned several valuable lessons back in June and were determined never to be caught on the back foot ever again. A period of relative stability followed this turbulent summer, but that simply meant that while the riots were behind us, we were still faced with the day to day problems and challenges that characterise prison work. As drugs were by now a constant issue and it was becoming obvious that Class A substances were entering the jail in increasing quantities, staff were always on the lookout for signs of abuse and constantly aware of the dangers of a prisoner overdosing, or consuming something toxic. The prison's dealers were 'cutting' (mixing) heroin with all kinds of substances to make their supply go further; talc and brick dust were two favourites, but we had no idea what else they might have been using.

One evening, in early 1989, I was called to the detail office. Along with another member of staff, I was told to provide an escort to Whitehaven hospital by ambulance. Staff had found a prisoner in one of the 'spam cans' who was totally off his rocker; one minute wild eyed and running towards the officers screaming "Grandad, Grandad" and the next, collapsed on the floor experiencing some kind of fit. All in all, most alarming. Staff had managed to restrain him and he had been taken to the segregation unit to await the ambulance. He was placed in the padded cell there, to be contained safely until the paramedics arrived. Meanwhile, our healthcare officer attempted to discover from him what he had taken, but to no avail. By now, he and his poor Grandad were deep in conversation and we were simply bystanders. When I arrived on the scene with my colleague, we found the prisoner laughing and then crying by turns, whilst curled up on the floor in a pool of sweat and urine. I have never before, or since, seen anyone sweat like that. He was a guy of about 50 years of age. Whatever he had taken was burning him up. We later learned that as a joke, he had been 'spiked' in his tea with LSD (Lysergic Acid Diethylamide, a psychedelic). It was with great difficulty that we were eventually able to place him on a stretcher. The ambulance crew strapped him securely down, whilst his body convulsed and he began shouting "hello, hello, hello", followed by a spell of screaming and a manic laugh. All the way to Whitehaven hospital he kept this up, arching his back and straining against the stretcher straps, till the floor of the ambulance was covered in his sweat. To this extent, the paramedic riding with us was concerned that a combination of the drug and dehydration might result in him suffering a cardiac arrest. On arrival at the hospital I don't recall what treatment he was given, but whatever it was, it settled him down somewhat. Following that and along with him, we were shunted off to a psychiatric unit, somewhere in Whitehaven or its environs, where we spent the night. It was a most miserable and dismal edifice which can have afforded little cheer to those confined there. I think and hope fervently that we offer better to our mentally ill these days. We were relieved by two more officers around 09.30 hrs next morning and I slept all the way home in their taxi. I saw the prisoner following his discharge back to us from the hospital and he remembered nothing of his 'trip' to Whitehaven. I told him what an exciting night he had missed.

As 1990 came around, Governor Lockwood left Haverigg, to be replaced by Governor Bernard Wilson, a free thinking and innovative gentleman who brought with him a like minded deputy, Brian Crosby. From the outset they began to encourage staff to develop various initi- atives. As a result Haverigg's Drug Rehabilitation Unit was established. In an area zoned off from the main prison, two billets housed between 20 and 28 volunteer prison- ers who wished to address their drug habits. The ethos being that the group would be mutually supportive, with the stronger among them provid-

Governor Wilson

ing encouragement to those who might fall by the wayside. The course was run by officers, who along with a psychologist formu- lated the course work. Classroom based, this involved intensive and sometimes rather confrontational group work. It was designed to show them how their drug use and criminal activities affected those close to them and the innocent victims they stole from to feed their habit.

We discovered that the amount of acquisitive crime necessary to keep some individuals supplied with their drug of choice was quite staggering. It's fair to say that in many ways we staff learned as much from the courses as the prisoners did. I worked in the rehab unit for some time and came to realise that it was not at all unusual for an addict to have a £400 to £600 weekly habit. If one takes into account that any stolen items would be sold for a mere fraction of their value, then the sheer volume of stolen goods and the cost to insurance companies is totally incredible. To a junkie, the ring or item of jewellery he steals from someone's bedroom dressing table equals a bag of smack, but to the victim who treas- ured the item, the loss is devastating and the violation of their home, heartbreaking and unsettling. On the occasion that we could drive this home to prisoners successfully, their discomfort was obvious. The overriding attitude of criminals is: you have, I take; it's insured, you make an inflated claim, just as I would; win-win situation. Salve for the criminal conscience, but honesty, morality and sentiment do not enter into it.

In late 1988, a young bloke fresh out of the Royal Marines was posted in to Haverigg. Officer Graeme Brass was a veteran of the Falklands conflict (amongst others) and like myself was a lover of the Lakeland fells. He and I hit it off straight away and so began a close friendship, which endures to this day. Graeme is an Alfred Wainwright fanatic who can quote from his fell guides in the same way that theologians can quote from scripture. He has always remained bitter about the fact that Eric Robson was chosen to present the Wainwright documentaries, firmly believing that it should have been him. So obsessed is he with AW that he once made a special trip to Kendal Museum, to see AWs pipe and a pair of his socks.

By the early 1990's, Graeme and I were working together a great deal and most of our leisure time was spent walking the fells. More often than not, along would come Officer Nicola Williams, one of a number of female staff, who were by then in post at Haverigg. Like all her fellow female colleagues, Nicola was extremely good at her job, possessed of a great sense of humour and seemingly boundless energy which earned her the nickname 'Tigger'. She was also extremely physically capable. I remember her once rugby tackling a prisoner much bigger than herself, to prevent him from escaping - our female staff were a formidable bunch.

CHAPTER ELEVEN

Tempus Fugit

From the moment I arrived at Haverigg, in the spring of 1978, I had been intrigued by its previous history as a Royal Air Force base, but had been unable to discover very much information about its wartime usage, or the aircraft that flew from its runways. Over the next 14 years, on more than one occasion, ex-RAF personnel would drop by our gate and enquire as to how much of the old base remained. It would have been lovely to have brought them in and have them explain all the old buildings to us, to reminisce about their service there during the war years. However, prisons in general remained very much 'off limits' to members of the public until the 1990's. Then the prison service seems to have decided that the public should be encouraged to see and judge for themselves our attempts at making best use of their money, in terms of rehabilitation and crime reduction.

For me in 1992 an opportunity presented itself which would change the course of my life and in the process, create a project which would touch the lives of many others, both in the prison and the broader community By 1992, HMP Haverigg had occupied the old airfield site for 25 years and Governor Wilson was seeking a suitable way to mark the occasion. A working committee was set up, of which I became part and various themes and attractions for the event were discussed. Governor Wilson had in fact served in the Royal Air Force before beginning his career in the prison service. Between us we decided that I would attempt to research the history of the site back to its origin as an airfield, we were both very enthusiastic but I had little idea how to set about this task other than that an appeal for photographs and recollections placed in various RAF publications might bear fruit and boy oh boy, was I right.

As word of my research began to spread I was approached one day by our prison boiler house engineer, Graham Brown, who showed me an artefact from an aircraft engine he had discovered whilst set line fishing off the beach, to the west of the airfield. Graham had no idea what type of engine it was, but informed me that it was located just below the low water mark, on the ebb of only the highest of tides and difficult to get to. Clearly, I needed to see this. I spent several tides wading around in my underwear (hold that thought), with no success. One early July morning at dawn and following the tide out to its lowest point, I finally spotted a section of the aircraft engine mounting frame, just visible above the water. After a quick investigation of the object attached to it, I established straight away beyond doubt that I was dealing with a radial engine which was half buried in the bottom of a shallow tidal gully. I decided there and then that if it was at all possible, then I should try to recover it.

In terms of knowledge and safety, it seemed to me that the best people to contact with regard to this task were Haverigg's excellent inshore rescue team. When I did so, they were most enthusiastic about the idea, pointing out an almost 10 metre tide on 2nd August as our best chance of success. The rescue team had just acquired an ex Army Stalwart amphibious vehicle and this was fitted with a hydraulic lifting crane. Using this machine a plan was hatched to drive out to the site just before low tide on 2nd August, put slings around what was exposed of the engine and try a gentle and straight extraction using the lifting arm of the vehicle. As I waited for the big day to arrive I set about trying to establish the origin of our engine. I had narrowed it down to three possible crashes offshore of the airfield. It was clear though that unless the engine still carried any identifying numbers, the mystery would remain unsolved.

The morning of the 2nd dawned wet and windy, as my team and I roamed off down the beach to snatch our prize and be back home in no time at all for bacon and eggs…wrong. As we all stood at the receding tide's edge, nervously looking at our watches and staring at the wave tops for a glimpse of mounting frame, the steady beat of the Stalwarts engine became a strangled sob and died, leaving us with only the sound of seagulls, wind and sea for company. All efforts to restart its huge Rolls Royce engine met with failure. Now engulfed by a gathering sense of disappointment and faced with a soon to be turning tide, we made a two mile dash back to inshore rescue HQ. A converted forklift truck was brought to tow the stricken machine away to safety. Upon arriving back at the scene and against all the odds, the forklift also broke down. Talk about despair.

As the tide continued to turn and advance, I could envisage myself being presented with a bill for the two vehicles and them being left to keep the aircraft engine company. However, after a manic ten or fifteen minutes and with the tide now lapping at our feet, the forklift was coaxed back to life and a very relieved but gloomy convoy began the retreat back to base (and the drawing board). The lads and lasses of Haverigg inshore rescue team do not readily accept defeat under any circumstances, but it still came as a bit of a shock when one of the team announced "No problem, I'll bring my JCB tonight and we'll dig it out." And do you know what? That's exactly what they did. No mechanical problems just dug it out, put chains on it and popped it ashore. Still with its propeller attached, it was without doubt an Armstrong Siddeley Cheetah. The story behind the aircraft, its crew and our restoration of it are told in my book, *A History of RAF Millom and the Genesis of RAF Mountain Rescue*, ISBN 978-0-9934679-9-8.

To cut a long story short, I managed to clean and restore enough of our recovered engine for it to form part of our autumn gala display of memorabilia relating to the history of RAF Millom. Our gala attracted several servicemen and women who had served at the airfield and was covered by our local paper, television and radio It was a huge success that raised enough money to make a sizeable contribution towards a station memorial, a huge slate slab with the recovered engine's propeller affixed to it was sited outside our Administration building following Governor Wilsons enthusiastic support for the project and at a full Staff parade for the dedication of our memorial we were overflown by 3 RAF Jaguars of No 6 Squadron courtesy of Governor Wilson's son a serving RAF Navigator with that Unit.

One of the proudest moments of my service, standing with the C\O of 14 MU Carlisle GRP\CPT Tim Leening in front of our station memorial.

By the end of 1992, we had from veterans and various agencies, a large amount of photographs, documents and artefacts in our possession which were clearly begging for a permanent home. Both Governor Wilson and I had the germ of an idea that this was the possible makings of a small museum, but where could we house our collection? Haverigg Prison Officers' Social Club occupied about half of the buildings that had once been the old RAF Officers' Mess. The other half was taken up by bachelor accommodation for prison staff which was no longer in use. One bright winter's morning I made a formal request to Governor Wilson that I be allowed to convert this now unused building into a suitable area to create our proposed airfield museum. He not only agreed to my request, but participated fully in the establishment and development of what became the RAF Millom Museum up to his retirement and beyond. The gutting of the building, the construction of display cases and the installation of photographic displays took place over the winter of 1992 and 1993. This was made possible by the help of volunteer colleagues who constantly 'dropped by' and selflessly gave of their time and energy.

At Easter 1993, the RAF Millom Museum opened its doors for the first time. The ribbon was cut by Pilot Officer David Waters of Hull, who served as RAF Millom's Senior Test Pilot from 1942 to 1944. For the first time also, the ex servicemen and women of RAF Millom gathered for their official reunion, some 100 strong. This first successful gathering was to set the trend for the years that ensued. Over 300 veterans from the UK and overseas would come together for their annual reunion. In doing so, our collection of photographs and artefacts would swell with each visit.

In late 1993 I became part of a project management team, headed by our Deputy Governor, Brian Crosby. The work was very interesting and rewarding. Among my many tasks I would prepare and deliver visual displays to Governors' regional conferences. This involved a good deal of photographic work around the prison, whilst also allowing me to use a portion of my time to field the increasing amount of correspondence I was receiving with regard to the museum project.

Haverigg now housed a significant number of life sentence prisoners. In acknowledgement of the fact that their social requirements differed somewhat from those of short term inmates, an unused WWII airmens' dining hall (formerly used as a cinema and television room) was being converted into a recreation centre, specifically for them. The task was being carried out by a single unsupervised prisoner, a lifer, a Scotsman called Archie Baillie. I was introduced to Archie whilst doing the rounds one morning with Brian Crosby and was greatly impressed by what he was achieving single handedly. Whilst with us at Haverigg, life sentence prisoners were assessed as to their suitability for progression through the system to a lower category establishment. Part of this was accompanied days out to experience other than institutional life. Some of these men had spent many years in prison, whilst the world outside moved on apace without them. Archie had become eligible for such a day out and had asked to go on a fell walk; a very welcome change from the usual "Can we go to Burger King Boss?" Myself and my pal Graeme agreed to take him and decided that as Archie had an interest in aircraft, we would take him to visit the Halifax bomber wreck site on Great Carrs, high up in the Coniston fells. The day was a great success, enjoyed by all three of us and though we did not know it, Archie and I would visit the Coniston fells again in the coming months.

In the process of preparing for the first RAF reunion, I had sought advice from David Reid and the team at the Dumfries and Galloway Aviation Museum. David and his crew run what is probably the best amateur aviation museum in the British Isles and my efforts were always based upon their excellent example. David knew that I was hoping to expand our collection, but also realised that we had very limited space at the time. Subsequently, when I got a phone call from him asking if I wanted my first aircraft, I was somewhat taken aback. "Don't worry though," he said, "you will have room for this one. It's a Flying Flea. But," he added, "it's in need of restoration, if you are up for it?"

The design of the Flying Flea was developed in the 1930's by a Frenchman named Henri Mignet . His dream being that anyone could build one of these little planes and take to the skies with minimal (or no) previous flying experience. Though Mignet and several others flew 'Fleas' successfully, many amateurs came to grief as the craze to build them gripped handymen everywhere. We believe that our HM14 is one of the earliest builds in preservation. We became so engaged with the history of Mignet's other designs that we would go on to scratch build a later variant, the HM280, in our prison workshop.

The story of Henri Mignet and his contribution to light aviation in a career spanning some 60 years is a long and rich one, told in the highly recommended book by Ken Ellis and Geof Jones, titled Henri Mignet and His Flying Fleas, ISBN 0-85429-765-0.

Henri Mignet at the controls of his Flea. Photo by permission from Ken Ellis

David gave me the contact details for Ken Ellis who is the country's foremost authority on this particular little aircraft and its variants. At the time he was also the editor of *Flypast* magazine. Ken was most entertained by the idea that a prison ran an Airfield Museum. He happily introduced us to Mrs Pennington who owned the aircraft which was currently stored in her barn, very close to us at Torver, near Coniston.

When I informed Governor Wilson that we had the opportunity to acquire and restore this little aircraft for inclusion in our museum, he was very much for the idea. However, we both suddenly realised that we were putting the cart before the horse. Could we restore it and where would the restoration be carried out? A visit was paid to Mrs Pennington's barn to see how much of the aircraft actually remained and to assess what sort of task we were faced with. The late Mr Pennington had acquired the Flying Flea complete with its V twin Anzani engine. Due to the reputation the type had gained for being extremely dangerous, he had very wisely elected not to attempt to fly it. Over the course of time he sold the Anzani engine and the family children used the fuselage as a toboggan, with predictable results. We found the two wings intact, but worse for wear with bird and mouse nests inside them, though the inhabitants had fled.

With no hesitation we announced that we could and would restore it to its original condition. The question of a workshop in which to do so resolved itself. Governor Wilson decreed that the lifer recreation room would be reduced in size and the remaining space given over for the rebuild of our 'Flea'.

As I could only devote my spare time to the restoration work, I needed a prisoner I could trust, one who was good at practical work in general and one who I could leave to work with only occasional supervision. It had to be Archie, who was already working in the building, if he was up for the job. After convincing him I was serious and that not only was the project a reality, but that he would be coming with us to pick up the aircraft, I left him smiling and shaking his head.

CHAPTER TWELVE

Everybody's Got a Hungry Heart
Bruce Springsteen

1994 was a turbulent year for me. I now had a full blown aircraft restoration project in hand and a growing museum to tend in addition to my regular duties. Still, it never seemed like a balancing act and I immersed myself in it totally.

My fell walking pal, Graeme, had taken a posting to HMP Durham which was closer to elderly family for him. That left Nicola Williams and I as walking partners, enjoying an increasingly warm friendship, which eventually spilled over into a love affair. Like many couples who marry young, my wife and I found that we had little in common after 22 years and I began to feel that we were both marking time until the kids left home and then what? So I became that cliché that I had always rolled my eyes at, the guy who has the workplace romance, leaves his family and sets up home with a woman 17 years his junior. It was not a decision I took lightly. Both my wife and I suffered a great deal of pain during the split, though it was not long after our separation that she found a new partner and started out on a second and happy marriage. This meant a move to Manchester for her and after some deliberation my son and daughter decided to stay in Haverigg with Nicola and I. John enjoys a very successful career at BAE Systems in the Barrow in Furness shipyard, Joanne served a number of years in the Royal Artillery completing more than one active tour of operations before leaving at the rank of Sergeant, and now runs her own confectionary and catering business also in Barrow.

127

For the next six years prison work consisted of the usual ups and downs. We now had a large cellular accommodation block, Residential Unit 1, consisting of two wings. I spent time working there and back on the drug rehabilitation unit, having completed my stint of the project management team. However, the real story of those years is the development of the aircraft restoration workshop and the RAF Millom Museum, so I make no apology for devoting this following chapter to that part of my story.

With the proposed workspace in the lifer centre now totally empty and ready to receive the Flying Flea, I needed to address the issue of transportation from Torver to Haverigg. However, this proved to be no problem at all. A team from the Dumfries and Galloway Aviation Museum came down with a large trailer and very expertly loaded the delicate components of the little aircraft, delivering it safe and sound to our new workshop. Ken Ellis was on hand to oversee the operation and it was the subject of our very first article in *Flypast* magazine.

We catch a flea and now the work begins
Archie and young Dumfries Museum helper loading the fuselage.

For Archie and I our first task was to assess the size and nature of the job which was ahead of us. Also, we needed to identify where we were going to obtain the tools necessary to set about it. As luck would have it, spare tools of various sorts were given to us from the prison's workshops. Additionally, I pitched in from my own pocket for any further items we could not beg (or steal). After a couple of weeks of preparation we were 'tooled up', to the extent that we could begin work.

With work well underway, both Archie and I began to realise that to complete the restoration; we would need the help of people who possessed the skills that we lacked, and so fully realising that the fuselage of the Flea would require a whole new plywood skin, we enlisted the expert help of the late Colin Dickinson who ran the woodwork classes in the education centre.

Colin had experience in aircraft building and was a superb craftsman. When we approached him, he was on board without hesitation. Due to his incredible workmanship, we were able to retain all the internal fuselage members which he reskinned beautifully, each panel with barely visible scarf joints. With everything going along well, Archie threw a spanner in the works over a brew one morning by asking.

"By the way, what are we going to cover the wings and rudder with?"

I said, "well, Irish linen is the correct material, but I will have to price a quantity of it. "

The cost turned out to be way beyond our non-existent budget, so we decided to see if the staff in the machine weaving shed could help us out. The manager there told us that they had produced a few sample rolls of light material very like the type of linen we were after for a contract that never came to fruition and that in so far as he knew they were still in the main stores. It is tough to get a storeman to release anything from a store ("stores are for storing, mate, sorry, no can do"), but on Governor Wilson's say so we obtained a big roll of this material, and it looked perfect. Back in the workshop, we decided to make up a wooden frame, cover it with this linen lookalike and see if it would shrink when coated in cellulose dope. Once again, Archie threw a monkey wrench into the cogs by pointing out that we did not have any cellulose dope.

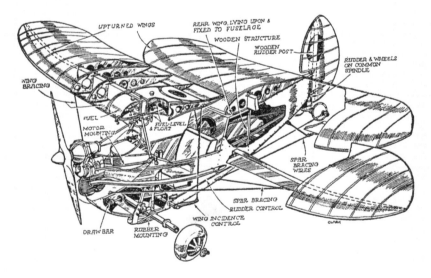

He was right, and sourcing it was not going to be as easy as sourcing the linen. A few days later, Governor Wilson came to the workshop to check on our progress, and I mentioned our problem to him. I don't know from where or how, but several days later, four one-gallon tins of cellulose aircraft dope were delivered to our workshop, much to our relief and delight.

The restoration was generating a lot of interest among our officers, and they would drop in from time to time to see how we were getting on. One afternoon we had a visit from a gentleman called Charlie Barr, Charlie was the Civilian instructor who ran the painting and decorating courses for prisoners, but he was also ex-Royal Air Force where he had served as a fitter and was familiar with applying fabric cover to an open airframe, would he help us? Yes, he would, and as he carried out the work, much of it in his own time, Archie and I became his apprentices.

We seemed to be crossing each bridge we came to reasonably easily. Still, the elephant in the room as we progressed was the fact that we did not have an engine for our Flea, a classic V twin of any description was again, way beyond our non-existent budget, and I was on the verge of looking for a scrap flat

Complete fuselage assessing wingfit and Archie starts work resetting wing ribjoints

configured engine from a VW Beetle which would have served our purpose, as we were restoring for static display only. Out of the blue a mechanic suggested using a Citroën 2CV engine, a two-cylinder engine also in flat twin configuration.

In Haverigg village was a Citroën dealership and garage run by Ian Hudson, so I decided to approach him and ask if he had such a thing as a scrap 2CV engine he could sell us?

He took me into his storeroom and pointed to a big pile of them, saying, "take your pick."

I did, and best of all, he gave it to us for free, this was fantastic , who needed a budget anyway.

Within a couple of days, we had the engine stripped of its cowlings, leaving it looking more like a motorcycle engine than something that drove a car, and our woodwork wizard was already at work carving a beautiful laminated propeller for us.

Now came the sourcing of suitable metal to recycle as brackets etc., and so Archie became a 'free range' scavenger around the jail, often prompting phone calls like this,

"Is that you, Nico?"

"Yes, what's up?"

"That bloody mad jock that works for you is climbing all over my scrap heap. Have you told him he can?"

My son John was security cleared to join us in the evenings in the workshop and carried out the cosmetic restoration of the 2CV engine prior to its installation on the airframe.

Archie is doing a quick calculation of how many materials we need to purloin to complete the rebuild.

"No, look, I will have a word with him, it won't happen again, ok?"

"Well, make sure you do. It's just not on, bugger me. He's just gone of carrying a load of tubing."

"Sorry mate, I will sort it, It won't happen again."

But it did, and this time I was truly complicit.

We needed two suitable wheels for the Flea, so the search was on. While on Farm fence patrol one day I came across a four-wheeled hand truck that didn't seem to be used much and had the wheels we so sorely needed. In an operation that would not have shamed the SAS, Archie and I 'liberated' two of its wheels and spirited them back to our workshop. It amazed us both that the theft was never mentioned and that nobody came looking for them with us the obvious suspects. Now emboldened, we broadened our scavenging activities to help us carry out our next restoration project, a vampire jet cockpit section that we purchased from the Dumfries Air Museum as surplus to their collection.

Looking good and check out the new wheels!

Around a week or so after the cockpit was delivered to our workshop, myself and a colleague were dispatched to a Young Offenders establishment over in the North East. We were to collect a young life sentence prisoner who had been reclassified as an adult and escort him back to Haverigg. As we made the return journey, I took a liking to the lad, he seemed a shy sort, but I drew him out a bit about what classes or courses he had taken during his sentence. It turned out that he had qualified from a general painting and decorating course. I asked him if he was interested in aircraft?

A bemused Colin sitting in his new project and pre restoration photograph of our Vampire T11 cockpit section and example of the aircraft it was taken from. Then Colin's beautifully restored cockpit section shown in our workshop and carrying No.6 Squadron crest which was hand painted and applied by our Governor Bernard Wilson, (did I mention that our Governor was a very talented artist ?) and finally at pride of place safe and sound in the RAF Millom museum.

"No", he replied," Not really."

"Have you done any metalwork or woodwork at all?"

"A little bit,"

"Can you use a spray gun?"

"Yes," he replied. "That was part of my painting course."

I was starting to have an idea that I might have another workshop recruit here bringing a new set of skills to our project. On arrival at Haverigg, I stayed with the young prisoner until the reception staff had processed him and then set off with him and his belongings for his allocated room. I asked him his name on the way, and he told me his surname.

"No, I said your Christian name?"

"Colin", he replied

"Right, Colin, we're going to make a bit of a detour; I want to show you something."

I took him into our workshop with the Flea almost rigged and complete, the jet cockpit on makeshift cradles behind it, and Archie hammering away at something or other, and gazing around he said

"What's this place?"

" I said its an aircraft restoration workshop"

"Who runs it?" He asked.

"Me and him," I said, pointing at Archie.

"Where's the officer?" He asked.

I said, "There isn't one unless one drops by."

I led him over to look at the Vampire cockpit and explained that it was to be restored to as near as pristine condition as we could get it, and would he like to take it on as his personal project? He looked astonished as he said,

"How would I do it if I don't know the first thing about aircraft?"

I told him, "Look, Colin, this is something you can do. You have 70% of the skills necessary. I will give you a cockpit manual for the Vampire and teach you the rest. It can take as long as it takes."

And so, from a closed and highly supervised environment to being offered a jet cockpit to restore with little or no supervision at all, Colin took to the job and he excelled at it.

We began to get visits from magazines, newspapers and radio who were all fascinated by what we were doing, and both Archie and Colin gave their own interviews. I remember Colin being very hesitant at first, but as time went on, his confidence and knowledge of the Vampire Jet made for a good interview.

We three would meet over coffee each morning and talk through the day's work, and maybe try and iron out any problems we might be having; in my absence, any decisions were taken by Colin and Archie, and their judgement was always sound. In addition to this, they never let me down from a security point of view either, their self conducted tool check was always correct, and any staff who dropped in to check on their progress always found them engaged totally in what they were working on and why not?

This was not the usual tedious, repetitive prison work; this was interesting, productive, unusual and enjoyable. It was a way to regain a little autonomy and self-respect and feel valued in a system where men often get lost and lose themselves.

Outside the jail, our museum was flourishing. A team of fellow officers and I began to make regular expeditions into the Lake District Mountains to recover artefacts from the many aircraft that crashed into the high ground during World War II. Two Epics spring to mind. The first was when a team, including Archie, climbed up into Cove Gill above Levers Water in the Coniston Fells to recover a large portion of Roll Royce Merlin engine from one of two Hawker Hurricanes that crashed there in 1943. We lashed the remains of the engine to a couple of wooden poles and carried it down –no mean feat, boy it was heavy.

The second epic recovery was that of the complete undertail section of the Halifax Bomber S for sugar which crashed on Great Carrs in 1944. This large piece of the airframe was located below the wreck site in Greenburn, above Little Langdale, and its recovery was an exhausting one carried out in foul weather conditions by a stalwart team of prison officers, heroes every one of them.

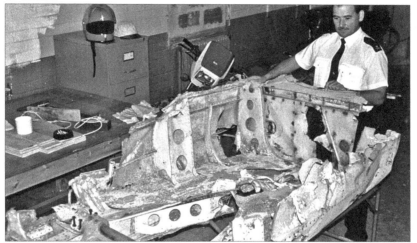

Undertail section from Halifax LL505 in the prison workshop
Later to be incorporated into a Halifax replica construction in Canada.

All amateur run museums need volunteers to function, develop, carry out maintenance, etc.,and many bring new and valuable ideas. During the museum's first year, a local man called Glyn Griffith came to the museum to offer his assistance which at the time was welcomed. However, in very short order, Mr Griffith brought his family and friends in with him and was soon a louder and more influential voice than my own with very different ideas about how things should be done. Though I did not realise it at the time, he was a 'Trojan Horse' who would be the architect of the RAF Millom Museum's destruction with the passive assistance of those he brought with him. However, that would be several years later, and hence beyond my control,but in his absence following the museum's demise I would be left to pick up many of the pieces and deal with the emotional fallout felt by veterans.

It did not take me long to recruit more lifers to the workshop though I kept the number to 4 or 5 to provide them all with project work. Archie saw the completion of his Flea project but was on the move, having fulfilled all the requirements to facilitate moving to a less secure establishment though this raised a real problem. Archie had a solid marriage, but visits were very difficult for his wife as their home was in Scotland. The prison service proposed transferring him to a prison in the South of England, which was ridiculous, so heads were gathered together. A far more sensible transfer into the Scottish prison system was facilitated as if by magic; everybody liked Archie. In the fullness of time, Archie would work for the Dumfries Air Museum on a day release basis and make several friends there before securing his parole. Now, after all the years and both out of our respective uniforms, he and I remain good friends, meeting when we can for a bar meal and a catch-up, usually sharing our scrapbook photos and workshop memories of the time with our wives.

It was via David Reid of the DAGAM that I heard of an Aviation Museum in Wales that was closing and had a Rolls Royce Avon Jet Engine for sale, so I immediately bought it for us; I mean, how could I not?

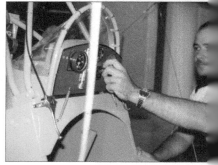

Archie makes a few last minute ri
adjustments then poses proudly with his
flea one last time before its departure
museum where the little aircraft along wi
cockpit became our two major exhibits.Att
to detail was always paramount to us and a
deal of care was given to the fleas cockp
instrument panel. I can be seen here wi
and starting its clock on arrival at the mu
for the very first time.

I bought it for a modest sum, however it had been left out in the elements and needed a lot of work, but I had just the boys for the job.

Ashburner's Fuel Supplies of Millom provided a Lorry for transportation, and now we had our very own Jet Engine to play with. At the same time, the Dumfries Aviation Museum loaned us an RR Kestrel Engine and a RR Merlin Engine, which needed a little work in their display stands, but that was what our workshop was about and now had two iconic exhibits for the museum.

Our Rolls Royce Avon jet engine prior to and after restoration. All cleaning and polishing was done by hand by a single member of our team and took three months.

In 1997 I married Nicola, my second wife, after three years together. My fell walking partner and wainwright devotee Graeme, unable to resist the lure of the mountains, took a posting back to Haverigg, and I bought a Helicopter, as you do.

I acquired the Westland Wessex chopper from Sunderland Air Museum for the princely sum of £375, and it was delivered to our museum yard by Bill Fern of the North Yorks Air Museum in several pieces, fuselage, rotorhead, rotor blades and tail boom though complete with its massive Alvis Leonides Major Radial Engine. Bill used his lorries' lifting gear to help us assemble it, and restoration was undertaken over many weeks by our prison workshop, Barrow Air Cadets and the Museum team.

This is the point at which you wonder if you may have bitten off more than you can chew.

Barrow Air Cadets and their C/O make their first visit to our now assembled Wessex helicopter.

Our completely restored Wessex helicopter right down to its pristine engine bay and just in time for our autumn RAF reunion.

Throughout the 1990s, Haverigg remained a lively place to work, to say the least and it was beginning to tell on staff with elevated levels of sick absence and mental health issues causing genuine concern for management. Haverigg was not unique in this. It was decided at national level that all establishments should have a dedicated care team to support staff who are struggling and carry out a critical incident debrief in the wake of a traumatic event such as suicide, assault or a violent incident. These teams consisted entirely of volunteer staff, and I agreed to form and lead the care team at Haverigg. I have always been proud of the work we did. Staff jokingly called us 'The Care Bears', but our support was rarely rejected. As one officer told me, "a breakdown is like a flying saucer; it's easy to be sceptical till you've seen one."

My friend Graeme and I worked together a great deal and had many adventures; these are two of the lighter ones. The first one had us escorting a young prisoner who was completely off his rocker with amphetamine psychosis to the psychiatric facility at HMP Wymott near Leyland in Lancashire. We were to travel by taxi, a journey of about two and a half hours. When we went to the medical centre to pick up the prisoner, we couldn't see what the fuss was about, and the lad was just sitting staring at the wall, calm as you please.

"Ah," our medical officer said, "you should have seen him fifteen minutes ago, but he's had an injection to settle him down."

"How long will that last?" We enquired.

"You won't hear a peep out of him till you get to Wymott", he replied, "that jab's good for over two hours, fellas."

Our journey went well until we got close to Forton Services on the M6, where all lanes ahead of us were jammed solid due to an accident further south. After a while, we began to creep along a short distance at a time, but it was evident that our journey would take much longer than anticipated, and we had already been on the road close to two hours. Our hospital officer was a bit out with his prediction. As the two-hour mark passed, sleeping beauty began to come to life, staring wildly around and becoming very agitated. It is a very strange thing, but the ramblings of those in the grip of this psychosis often have a religious element, and this proved to be the case with our fellow passenger. As he became more agitated, he began straining forward and telling our driver not to worry because he knew who he was and that he knew where he was taking us because our taxi driver was none other than Moses. Very soon, he was talking 50 to the dozen about how Jesus was with us and that we were not to worry about a single thing because it was all part of the plan and everything was taken care of. This did nothing to calm myself or Graeme, putting us increasingly on edge, and our terrified taxi driver had slid himself so far down in his seat that only his head was visible. I decided that the best course of action to take in the circumstances would be for me to join in with the madness, and so that's what I did. The prisoner and I gleefully cherry-picked characters and stories from the new

141

and old testaments, both agreeing that all would be well and that 'Moses' would get us safely to our final destination, which happily for us all, he did. After dropping the lad off at Wymott, both Moses and Graeme complimented me on an outstanding performance adding that it was so accomplished that it was hard to tell which of us was the nutter.

Our second noteworthy adventure was on the occasion when we were called by radio to remove a prisoner from the tailor's workshop who was causing problems, straight forward enough job, pick him up and locate him in the seg unit, no trouble.

One of Graeme's favourite pastimes is baiting me about my knowledge of the wainwright fell guides, and as we made our way to the tailor's shop, I was subjected to "what did AW say about the Howgills?"

I said, "he thought that they resembled sleeping elephants. Now give it a bloody rest, will you."

As we entered the workshop, we were confronted by the cleaner who had already thrown a full dustbin through the office window and was now swinging a shovel at us.

Dialogue and persuasion are by far the most powerful tools employed by prison staff. Contrary to what many believe they are deployed much more often than physical restraint and to more significant effect As we escorted our now compliant prisoner to the seg unit, having succeeded in getting him to surrender his shovel and come quietly, I couldn't resist asking Graeme with a grin, "I wonder what AW would've said about all that then?"

He replied, "AW would've said that we would both have been better employed sitting up on Haystacks."

CHAPTER THIRTEEN

Bad moon rising

Creedence clearwater revival

In 1998 a series of events took place in the prison and the museum. A complete change for the aircraft restoration workshop came about with the retirement of Governor Wilson and the transfer of his deputy Brian Crosby, both of whom had been supportive of my project and actively involved in a practical way from the outset. The man to replace Bernard Wilson was to be Governor G.Brunskill. The latter, along with our new Deputy Governor, viewed the unsupervised aircraft workshop in a different light, and it was not long before a civilian instructor was recruited to staff it.

To my mind, this negated the whole ethos of the experiment, which had been up to that point a complete success. However, the instructor they chose was an old school friend of mine, Rick, a guy who could turn his hand to anything, which made things easier and more so because, at this point, I was in the middle stages of a really ambitious project. Having successfully restored an HM14 flying Flea, it had been on my mind for a while that we should attempt to scratch build one of Mignets many other designs but which one?. I had decided on the HM 280 of WW2 vintage.

In 1944 as the allies slowly began to advance through occupied France, Henri Mignet was contacted by Colonel Eon of the resistance movement who needed a small aircraft capable of sneaking its pilot behind enemy lines, a machine which could land and take off from a very small area and could be easily hidden. Mignet rose to the challenge, and thus the HM280 was born.

With its folding wings and steerable undercarriage, the little plane was more than fit for purpose, and it was planned to put the type into production after the war, but following the German surrender, these plans were abandoned.

Mignet preps the HM280 for flight and the little aircraft on the move with the French Resistance. *Photos courtesy of Ken Ellis*

Eon's HM280 survived the war and became part of the Musee L'air collection held at Le Bourget near Paris, where sadly it was destroyed during a fire there some years ago, the only one of its kind. I decided that this would be the design that we would attempt to replicate, but obviously, there would be no plans available, and it was unlikely that we could work from the only three surviving photos we had of the type. Help and a revelation came to us via the writings of Ken Ellis, which informed us that a variant of the HM280, was built after the war by Mignet and other enthusiasts. It also had folding wings. It was not at all unlike its predecessor but would we be able to source any plans? I decided to put out an appeal and was astonished when I received an almost immediate reply. As a result, a gentleman in Belgium had a 280 plan, and yes, he would be more than happy to send us a copy. Now we could begin, or could we?? When the plans arrived, all notation was in French. However, our workshop was full of various talents, and one of our number was fluent in the language and soon had us off the starting blocks.

Meanwhile, on the domestic front, my wife and I had moved house from Haverigg and relocated to a lovely converted farmhouse with barns near Kirksanton. The property came with an acre of land, some of which was quite wet and was bordered on one side by a large reed bed. We decided to give over a third of the acre to a fishing pond, a project that we both enjoyed, not least of all because of the abundance of wildlife it attracted, and life was good for us there, though problems were beginning to manifest themselves at the museum.

A move to Kirksanton and two new and lovely additions to our lives, our Airdale puppy Hamlet and my very own fishing pond, every anglers dream!

I was always acutely aware that my museum occupied prison service property and as such it was my sole responsibility to ensure that the buildings and outside areas were kept clean, tidy and uncluttered at all times. To this end, I had a strict policy of never obtaining or accepting a potential exhibit (with the obvious exception of the helicopter) unless we could house it safely and dry within the museum. It seems that my volunteer team decided that this was impeding the rapid growth they felt we should aspire to. The aforementioned Mr Griffith, now a far more influential voice than my own, decided to take matters into his own hands. Without my knowledge and with no consultation, he purchased several large items and had them delivered to the yard area of the museum. Among these items were two vampire wings, two Vampire tail booms, a derelict Vampire NF10 cockpit which was little more than a metal frame and a Jet Provost cockpit which required a little TLC but was far too good to sit out in the weather.

I took exception to this unexpected turn of events, not least of all, because it was evident that I had not got a clue what was being decided out of my sight and hearing. Clearly, I could hold as many meetings as I wished, but the real decisions were being made elsewhere.

I made my feelings very clear though perhaps not forcefully enough. Still, it resulted in Mr.Griffith refusing to come to the museum for a week, during which time I had the Provost cockpit taken into the prison workshop for a tidy up while I made space for it in the museum. Having done this in good faith, I expected the matter to blow over, let bygones be bygones and move on in the understanding that it was not to happen again. It came as a shock then when I was summoned to Governor Brunskill's office and told that Mr.Griffith had written to him claiming that I had misappropriated a piece of property that belonged to him, this being the Provost cockpit and had done so without his permission. I was absolutely stunned by this news and explained the situation before giving my assurances that I would resolve the matter straight away. I did this by meeting with Mr.Griffith and his family and eventually clearing the air. Still, it was apparent from the lack of support for me shown by the other team members that the balance of power was shifting. My influence was decreasing steadily. With the care team and prison duties added to this, what had been a pleasure was fast becoming a tiring and almost constant source of stress.

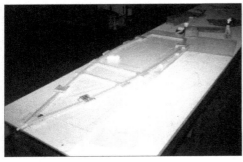

The outline of the HM280 fuselage is laid down and construction of the internal structure is shown here, the skinning of the fuselage was carried out in much the same way as with the HM14.

In the prison workshop, the construction of the HM280 was progressing exceptionally well. The team under Rick's guidance had begun making all the metal hinges and fittings for the plane from scavenged and recycled metal. On the separate set of workbenches, the complex wings were under construction by two men dedicated specifically to that part of the build. I had always employed a small team in the workshop and always lifers

The amount of time and effort involved in making all the ribs and assembling the two wings was enormous, my lads told me that they began to dream about wing ribs in their sleep.By the time we had completed the wings we were glad to put the task behind us but were mightily proud of what we had achieved.

We decided to virtually complete the fuselage before we began construction of the wings and all components such as the steerable undercarriage units and cockpit controls were hand crafted from recycled metal by the team.

who had the sentence time with us to truly invest in our projects and who would peer teach their replacements before they moved on through the system, but in late 1998 it was decided to double the number of men in the workshop and that for the first time short term prisoners would be employed in there. I was not at all happy about this. Still, the matter was out of my hands. My main concern was for the safety of the artefacts awaiting restoration. Sadly, my fears were justified as graffiti began to appear around the workshop. It was evident from the attitude of several short term prisoners that the whole ethos of the project was dissolving before my eyes. Still, my lifers were as committed every bit as much as me to the HM 280 project and the excellent quality of their work never faltered.

After a week's leave, I visited the workshop to check on progress and found three washing machines in a dismantled state between two benches. It transpired that Rick had volunteered to repair them and any others on a rolling basis in my absence. Still, worse was to come; he had decided along with the industrial manager that the shop should diversify and that from the end of that month, would begin to manufacture wrought iron gates and railings. I was speechless in the face of this news and knew from that moment that my workshops days in its original form were numbered and that once again, a monumental decision had been made in my absence. As I turned to leave the workshop, I saw scratched deep into an artefact on one of the benches, , 'MACCA OV BOOTLE' and' MANCS ON TOUR', clearly, the writing was also, on the wall.

The HM280 was completed in January 1999. In terms of Museum projects on that scale, it was to be our swansong with the workshop increasingly being given over to all manner of unrelated industries. However, the occasional job was done for the museum, which was invaluable to me as we had no workshop facility to speak of on the premises. January was also when HMP Haverigg received its prestigious Charter Mark award. Still, it was only a scant four weeks later, on Valentine's day, the 14th of February, that 200 prisoners rioted, setting buildings alight and causing a significant amount of damage. There would be no wining and dining with my wife that evening. We spent it behind flak shields. At one point, my wife turned to me and said, "God! This is romantic, isn't it?"

I would have preferred the alternative and told her so.

Later that same year, I found out that I had been nominated for the prison service Butler Trust award for my project work with prisoners and the establishment of the RAF Millom Museum and its annual reunion. I was surprised and heartened by this as I felt that what I had built perhaps might be guaranteed a secure future being formally acknowledged as it now was. After attending an interview in Westminster, it was announced some weeks later that I was to receive the award at Buckingham Palace in the new year of 2000 along with others whose work in various areas was being recognised. My wife and I enjoyed the event immensely. We attended a dinner hosted by Terry Waite on the evening before the awards ceremony and next day I was presented with my award by Princess Anne followed by an informal buffet lunch, heady stuff for a lad from the sticks.

Two weeks after returning from London, I was called into the Governor's office to be informed that my prison workshop was to be closed permanently on health and safety grounds as it was considered a fire risk. I was utterly taken aback by the news and not prepared for it from a practical point of view as it would involve me clearing the building entirely and finding space at the museum to store all of the items. The situation was fraught, and it did rather take the shine off my award, leaving me wondering if perhaps I had been given a warm drink before they put me to bed?

As the months of the new century came and went I was finding it more and more challenging to maintain a balance of long shifts at the prison and overserving my authority with regard to the museum, I knew full well that I was becoming seen as superfluous by the museum team and that my efforts to temper a headlong rush to expand by emphasising the fact that too much too soon could spell disaster was seen as obstructive.

A proud moment as I was asked by Princesse Anne, ``how many years of hard labour does this represent then?" and outside the Palace with my wife following my award.

Amateur aviation museums were folding all over the UK and our geographical location placed us at a disadvantage in terms of visitor numbers though this was offset to some degree by our autumn reunions which generated sufficient income from donations etc to help sustain us through the coming year, and our museum shop supported things a little further and so I felt that in terms of the premises we occupied and in order to keep things neat, tidy,

'e decided unanimously to go with a camouflage
ish for the HM280 which left us looking then for
engine. We managed to scavenge a 2 stroke motor
m an old generator which once installed with yet
other superbly carved propeller from the late Colin
ckinson allowed us to begin the complete assembly
our aircraft.

By now the team were quite well versed in the
art of linen covering our airframes and could
achieve a drum tight finish without warping
flying surfaces as can be seen here.

Our completed HM280, scratch built by an unlikely team in an unlikely location
with my then wife Nicola overseeing final rigging before its despatch to our
museum.

clean and presentable with the exception of any further small
donated exhibits we almost had a complete museum and from
then on it was about quality and not quantity, with the emphasis
on providing a positive visitor experience.

My wife Nicola was one of the most capable members of staff I
ever worked with and never gave less than her best in any given
situation. Still, after ten years of service, she decided on a change of
career; we were both becoming unhappy with the job, but Nicola
was the one with the University qualifications and I was caught

in the pension trap with only about six years till retirement and so we decided that regardless of salary, she should be the one to leave. Still, we both realised that it would probably mean leaving our large property at Kirksanton and moving to a house that would be financially manageable following a potential drop in income for us.

We quickly sold our property at Kirksanton and bought a house on the Croftlands estate in Ulverston, which had a good-sized garden and a spacious garage that provided me with a fine workshop to pursue my hobbies. Not long after moving there, Nicola left the prison service and began work at St Martin's college in Ambleside, which meant that we both had equal distances to commute to work, and we quickly settled into our new routine.

After 27 years of service and for the very first time, I began to feel a reluctance to go to work, coupled with episodes of mild anxiety at times which was totally out of character for me and realising that whilst alcohol was providing a quick but temporary fix most evenings I had the good sense to realise that it was fueling the negative state of mind I was in. I quit drinking for over a year, but the cracks were still there, and I knew it.

Throughout 2001 Haverigg prison experienced a relatively high level of prisoner on prisoner violence, though now, for the first time, staff were occasionally being assaulted too. Most of the violence among the prisoners was drug-related over unpaid debts, and each gang of suppliers usually had an enforcer who would be vicious and violent enough to instil the fear of God into victims to the extent that following even an injurious and serious attack by him they would never reveal his identity under pain of death.

I well remember one such enforcer, a scarred and evil-looking individual with the most deformed hands I have ever seen; they looked as though they had been hit repeatedly with a sledgehammer, he had made quite a name for himself in the prison but finally overstepped the mark when he hospitalised a young prisoner who was persuaded to bring charges against him. The young lad did not know the name of his assailant and so one of our assistant Governors decided that the best course of action would be to bring the suspected attacker and victim together under escort to an empty dining hall where the young lad could identify him. None of us escorting staff thought this advisable, and when the lad was told of the idea, he was clearly terrified at the prospect, but management is usually correct, aren't they? I mean, that's why they hold elevated positions isn't it? What could go wrong? Myself and another officer brought the young lad, who was clearly almost on the verge of tears, to the dining hall where our assistant Governor informed him that the man suspected of carrying out the attack on him was to be brought for him to positively identify and 'did he understand?' to which the lad nodded nervously.

Next in came mangled hands with his two-man escort looking very much the part and fixing his victim with a malevolent stare which carried the clear message 'don't you fucking dare put the finger on me.' The lad was asked, "Is this the man who attacked you?" But he did not reply, which agitated our Assistant Governor who demanded, "Is this the man?"

"Yes." Blurted out the young prisoner nervously.

At which his attacker broke free from his escort and ran at the lad, roaring, "I'll rip your fucking face off you fucking grass."

Instinctively myself, and my colleague put ourselves between the two prisoners, and the other escorts grabbed mangled hands and attempted to restrain him. Still, once again, he broke free and ran towards the double doors through which he had been brought.

At the top of each of these doors was a 12-inch square panel of wired safety glass, and without pausing, and in a move that defied credibility, he punched his right fist through one of them. Not content with that and all the while screaming 'Fuck you!' He began rotating his wrist around the jagged hole in a spray of blood and threatening to do the same with his left fist if anyone came near him. I was dispatched from another door to try and immobilise his hand from outside, and by the time I got to him, there was a cascade of blood down the door and a growing pool of it below.

We needed to de-escalate the situation fast and so we set about trying to reason with him, some ten minutes or so later, and not least of all, I think because he was feeling the effects of blood loss, he agreed to allow us to extract his hand and treat his wounds. At no point during the incident did he give any sign of feeling pain and throughout exhibited nothing but rage; had I not witnessed what he did, I would not have thought it humanly possible though given the state of his hands it was evident that it was not the first time they had seen such usage.

In the prison service, just when you think that you have seen it all - you haven't. An hour after completing my report on the dining hall incident, I was back on my wing and being informed by my senior officer that he had a job for me, I asked what it was, and he said, "I need you to take a prisoner over to health care to let them have a look at him."

"What's up with him?" I asked.

"Oh, it will be better if he tells you himself," he said with a grin.

When we got to the lads' cell, there was the young fella, a lad with learning difficulties, sitting on his bed looking healthy enough to me, and grinning like the Cheshire cat.

"What's wrong with you, son?" I asked.

"Cant piss, boss", he replied.

"Tell officer Nixon why you can't piss," said my senior officer.

"I've glued my cock, boss," he said with a toothy grin.

I asked him to repeat this, at which he offered to show me his handy work, and before I could decline his offer, all was revealed, and yes, he had well and truly cut off his plumbing.

"Why did you do this?" I asked him.

"The lads in the workshop bet me a half-ounce of baccy that I wouldn't do it." He said.

"Fair enough", I replied, "what did you use?" I asked

"No nails, boss," he replied proudly.

"And did you get your half ounce?" I asked.

"Yes, boss", he beamed.

"Well," I said, "it's off to health care for you best not 'stick around here."

After a trip to Furness general hospital, he was back on the wing, happy as a clam and with the forever nickname of no nails. You laugh, or you would weep. There are those who do not belong in prison but are placed there in spite of the prison service having nowhere near the means necessary to engage with them and carry out the work and support that they so sorely need.In a time when services are cut to the bone prison remains the easy option for the courts.

By 2002 my wife was very happy in her new job, making new friends and enjoying the social life of St Martins College whilst at 49 years of age, I was seriously beginning to wonder if I could, in fact, complete a further six years in the prison service. I had a long drive to work (20 miles each way), the shifts I was working were variable and sometimes very long; in fact, it was not uncommon to complete a 12 hour shift and then have to escort a sick prisoner to hospital where you would remain until you were relieved the next morning.

As head of the prisons Staff care team, I found myself visiting an increasing number of staff in their homes to offer support following them being signed off on sick leave due to stress, burnout, breakdown etc, and as the rights and entitlements of prisoners increased and the pressures of operational requirements mounted upon us, I was not faring much better myself. Following a particularly harrowing home visit during the late summer, I returned to my car and, looking at myself in the rearview mirror, said aloud, "Am I heading in the same direction?" It seems I was.

As summer turned to autumn, I felt constantly tired, increasingly anxious in crowded places, struggling to concentrate on even the most simple task and with a mind that woke me at 3 am each morning fizzing with every worry in the world. My wife and I had booked a holiday to the Canary Islands, which should have been a break to look forward to. Still, as the time got nearer, I became more and more afraid of the prospect of boarding a plane full of people and enduring the 4 hour flight.

Two days before our departure Nicola and I went shopping at Tesco in Barrow in Furness for some last-minute items to take on the trip. While shopping there, I experienced my first full-blown anxiety attack, breathlessness, chest pains, and a feeling of blind panic came over me from absolutely nowhere. My wife realised what was happening and we quickly grabbed our shopping and returned to our car, where I managed to settle myself a little for the journey home but on the way there I suffered a truly massive anxiety event to the extent that had the car been stationary I would have simply jumped out and blindly ran away such was my panic.

I have tried to explain what it felt like to people on occasion. The best description I can give is this when one has a tooth cavity and bites into a sweet, the tooth begins to ache straight away, but you know that the pain will build until it plateaus and then will recede, with a panic attack, the fear builds and builds to the point where you think your mind will break. You are in a terrible situation because the organ, the very thing that will tell you that your panic will recede, has gone rogue on you.

By the time we arrived back at the house, I knew that there was no way on earth that I could go on holiday, but I insisted that my wife should and so my plane tickets were changed into my daughter's name and I was left to sort myself out. My first port of call was my GP, who could quickly see that I was on the rocks and I was prescribed antidepressants, given a sick note for a month and told to go home and rest. My second trip was to the local kennels to apologise for changing plans and bring our airedale terrier Hamlet home with me. Aside from him, I have never wanted to be alone more in my entire life, and he was the perfect companion. For a whole week, I hardly ate and slept very little, instead walking through the night with my canine shadow, occasionally I would meet a fellow wanderer sometimes at 2, 3 or 4 am, and we might exchange a few words, those nights taught me a lot about mental health, there are many troubled souls out there unseen and unnoticed.

During that week, my wife made several worried phone calls to see how I was, and the odd one I answered must have made it plain to her that I was just about round the bend, even I knew I was spouting garbage. By the time she came home, I was starting to get on a more even keel, but I am sure that the lead up to my breakdown and the actual event did the first real damage to my marriage, I must have been hard work to live with during that time. For six months, I remained on sick leave but all the while, knowing that after that period was over, my pay would be halved unless I returned to duty. Before that could happen, however, I had to attend an interview with a psychiatrist down in Manchester to confirm I was no longer nuts. He asked me a good number of probing questions and finished by saying, "your GP said that you presented as being passively suicidal, Mr Nixon. Did you think of killing yourself?"

"No," I replied, "not myself, just other people."

At which he made a note on my file. Bloody hell, I thought. I hope he realised that was a joke, or they will nut me off for good. Whatever it was he wrote, back to work I went but with little enthusiasm.

CHAPTER FOURTEEN

So begins another weary day
Madness

I remember 2004 as the beginning of a boring unfulfilling endgame to my service as I found myself after almost three decades of experience doing little more than counting prisoners, giving out newspapers and mail, carrying out routine patrols and supervising dining and association areas. These duties are, of course, the mainstays of the prison regime. Still, in the wake of my project management work, running drug rehab courses and the incredible achievements of my workshops lifer team, they were the equivalent of sitting in a darkened room singing ten green bottles over and over all day long.

This was also the year that I decided to cede control of the museum to the volunteers. It had always been my intention to do so when I felt that the time was right. Also, it seemed appropriate that the museum should be run by a community-based team rather than be tied to the prison service, and so I stepped down and handed control to the team but agreed to continue my research on their behalf.

Very quickly, Mr Griffith appointed himself head of the organisation and like it or not, now that my influence (such as it was) was removed from the equation, it was evident that things were going to be done very differently from that point on. Though I had some grave misgivings about that, I was as good as my word in stepping down and resolved myself not to interfere.

158

That early Summer, I was sitting at my computer one morning quietly and steadily going out of my mind whilst trying to sort out a prisoners canteen order for him when I got a call from my pal Mick Purvis our reception officer, "Hey Nico" he said, "You need to come down here and meet an old acquaintance of yours, he's just come in on the Strangeways draft . "

"Who is it?" I asked.

"No," he laughed, "you need to come down here; he's an old, old adversary."

When I arrived at reception, I asked, "Come on, who is it, Mick?"

"He's in the waiting room; we left him till last so you two could get reacquainted."

I opened the door and peered inside to find none other than John Brooke, the Barns murderer, regarding me balefully with his one good eye.

"Remember me?" I asked him.

"No, You all look the fucking same to me."

"Fair enough," I said and closed the door.

Returning to the reception desk, I found Mick with Brooke's record open in front of him at the page showing my adjudication report from Gartree, "bloody hell Mick" I said, "the guy doesn't belong here; he's a stone killer, he even threatened to kill me."

"I'm not surprised," said Mick" you cost him a lot of time down the block, anyway; he's a model prisoner now apparently, even taken up art in a big way.

Brooke remained with us without incident until just before my retirement when he suffered a heart attack and was sent elsewhere. I was astonished; I didn't believe he possessed that particular organ.

In any prison and at any time, a violent fight between prisoners can occur and will almost always require staff to intervene. Fistfights are bad enough, but where weapons are involved, the incident must be brought to an end as swiftly as possible and hopefully without injury to officers or prisoners. Officer Dave Smith and I were on duty on the programmes unit one night just after evening meal, taking applications from prisoners for various things whilst two men were playing pool outside the office. We suddenly heard a row in the pool room, and before we knew it, the two pool players had smashed their cues in half and were using the thick ends as clubs knocking the living daylights out of each other. It all happened so fast that we did not have time to push the alarm bell, and Dave was the first to wade into the fray to try and separate them. I was right behind him, and it was apparent that these lads meant each other serious harm over some beef or other. Each man was receiving heavy blows to the head and shoulders, and they were only narrowly missing us too as they clubbed and flailed at each other, by now outside our office door. Dave managed to push Prisoner B back against the wall and hold him there. I forced Prisoner A against the doorframe and pinned his weapon arm with my right arm, all the while shouting "enough, enough", but he continued to struggle until quite suddenly the fire went out of him, and he nodded "ok."

"Drop the bloody cue." I said.

Which he did, but his eyes looked glazed, and he didn't seem quite with it. Dave had radioed for assistance by this time, and staff were beginning to arrive with us. Both prisoners were taken to the segregation unit, where prisoner A began causing problems before collapsing and suffering a cardiac arrest, On duty in the seg unit, that night was my pal Graeme Brass who fought for thirty minutes to keep the guy alive until the paramedics arrived to take over, performing CPR and resuscitating him no less than three times. Some days later, the two men were being processed in reception pending transfer; as prisoner B was leaving, he said to the officer there, "please tell Mr Brass thank you for not letting

160

that bastard die; I would've been on a murder charge otherwise, tell him I'm grateful."

As Prisoner A was about to leave, he was asked, "Do you have a message for Officer Brass ?"

"Who the fuck's he?" Asked A.

"He's the officer who saved your life."

To which the prisoner snorted dismissively and replied," He was only doing his fucking job; it's what he's paid for innit?"

There are those in the system for whom life is cheap, even their own.

CHAPTER FIFTEEN

It looks like I'm up shit creek again
Tom Waites

There can be no doubt that I was taking my frustrations and negativity home with me to a young wife. She, by contrast, was upbeat and happy in her new job. So it should have come as no surprise to me that my marriage was suffering as a result by late summer that year. Still, in early October, when my wife told me that our relationship was not working and that she wanted me to move out of our home, I was utterly devastated. I had been so caught up in my own unhappiness that I had not realised the impact that it was having on her.

There was to be no reconciliation, and so I moved out almost immediately and rented an apartment in Ulverston, taking little with me but my clothes and a few essentials where I found that the previous tenant had very thoughtfully left their successor a table, a broken chair and a busted fridge freezer, not a very august manner in which to begin a new life. My son and daughter quickly rallied around, and I soon had a bed, pots, pans, linen, etc and over the following weeks I slowly began to build a home for myself, but I was far from happy and dreading Christmas.

My late sister-in-law Lesley from my first marriage and I were extremely close, enjoying a brother and sister relationship that was unshakeable. Les always knew what was best for me and was never shy about telling me what it was. In early December, she announced that she had set me up on a date with a woman who would be the perfect company for me as "it was no good just moping; I needed to get on with my life." Her husband, Mike and his father ran a carpet fitting business in town, and the venue for this date was to be their annual Christmas dinner. I wasn't very enthusiastic about the prospect, nor was my proposed date. Her name was Philippa, a very slim, attractive blonde lady who I remembered from many years before when she and her ex-husband ran the Piel Castle public house in Ulverston.

Once introduced, we hit it off straight away and found that we had an incredible amount in common; her ex-father in law had been cook and baker at Gartree prison just before I was posted there, and she had attended one of my RAF reunions with her late mum because her father, who she lost when she was only five years old not only served at RAF Millom but was a founder member of the RAF mountain rescue service there.

"What do you do for a living?" I asked.

"I'm a house and animal sitter," she said.

"Never met one before", I replied, "must be interesting."

"You have no idea" was the reply" she already knew what I did for a living and echoed ", that must be interesting too."

To which I reciprocated by also laughing and saying, "you have no idea."

At the end of the evening, I was invited back to her flat for coffee where I was warned in no uncertain terms there was to be no impropriety whatsoever no matter how drunk I might be and afterwards, I left with her phone number and a firm promise that we would see each other again. It was the start of what has been a long, eventful and happy journey for us both.

By the spring of 2005, I was joining Philippa at her various house and animal sits when my prison work allowed and whilst recovering from a minor operation, I went out to Portugal for a while where she was taking care of a Villa, I was beginning to see what retirement might look like though it was some way away.

In June that year, my mother, who had been suffering from heart failure for some time, died suddenly, which meant a huge life change for me. My father was not in the best of health and utterly bereft at the loss of mum, and I felt that I had no alternative but to move in with him and take on the role of carer. The situation was made easier for me by Philippa, who would drop in and cook a meal for him if she was working nearby, and Dad adored her company. From High Newton to Haverigg and back meant a 60-mile round trip, and a late shift would see me getting in at around 10 pm and often leaving for an early start at 6 am the following day. With an apartment in Ulverston which I kept on but only used occasionally, caring for my father, long hours travelling and the job itself, I am afraid that the whole year became a blur to me and has become even more so with the passage of time.

However, I do recall one incident that year, which upset me more than any of the violence, injury, and disorder I had witnessed in my entire service. It involved a young scouse prisoner who gave us nothing but trouble; if there was a fight to be had, then he was in it, and he was continually abusive to staff into the bargain. No matter how hard you tried, it was impossible to build a rapport with him. He seemed to be just plain angry all the time. One morning he reported sick to the healthcare centre with severe stomach pains and was rushed to hospital with appendicitis. Another officer and I were his escorts, and there was little in the way of conversation on our journey. After seeing him off to the Operating theatre, we sat waiting for him to be brought back to a side room off the main ward. I knew he would still be out cold when he came back, and sure enough he was and so told my opposite number to nip down to the hospital canteen for a brew and a snack. Some 10 or 15 minutes later the lad started to come around and what followed will stay with me for the rest of my life as he began sobbing and pleading "No, No, I don't want to!" and for the next few minutes he relived a violent sexual assault upon himself by an adult who he called Sir all the while crying and moaning "It hurts!"

I have never been closer to hugging a prisoner in my life and was close to tears myself. I went and stood outside his room until he was fully conscious and back to his usual truculent self, but I never saw him in the same light after that.

Research into his record told me that he had been put into the North Wales 'care' system at a very young age, and several homes in that system came in for a great deal of scrutiny and criticism around the time that I was about to retire following stories of physical and sexual abuse from those young people who had been residents there, indeed prosecutions and custodial sentences resulted. In a brief snapshot, I had seen the frightened, helpless, broken and permanently damaged little boy who would become the angry, violent young man. It gave me pause to ponder what sort of society 'rescues' children from chaotic, dysfunctional and often violent domestic situations, then places them into the hands, and at the mercy, of predatory serial abusers. People who are allowed to engage in that activity for years without intervention from social services or any overseeing body – who should in a sane and humane world be safeguarding the welfare of these vulnerable young people.

As the year drew to a close, I started to look for a way out of the prison service. The crunch came in the spring of 2006 when Philippa sat me down and laid it on the line. I was tired, not giving work my full attention and realising once again that I was carrying the job around with me outside of work hours. I knew that I could take early retirement after having served 32 years, but I simply put that idea on the back burner until the new year.

She said," Look, you're tired, you're not giving anything or anyone your best; I'm afraid it's either the job or me, your choice. "

The choice was easy; I began to look at my pension and final gratuity and how reduced it would be if I retired two years early which turned out to be quite a lot a lot. I would lose about a quarter of both because of how the civil service pension scheme was set up, but I didn't care. I would get a part-time job if necessary. All I wanted to do was get out, and I chose my birthday, August 3rd to make my escape.

I spent the night before with Philippa in Coniston, where she was looking after a nephew's house. The following day she drove me to work for my final shift, which I spent saying my goodbyes to everyone before marching smartly to the gate lodge, all the while whistling to the theme tune from the great escape before handing in my keys and radio for the very last time.

Some dread retirement and a sense of disorientation can follow for them. In contrast, for others like myself, there is nothing but a feeling of relief at the chance to begin an entirely new chapter of one's life, not an end to anything but a beginning. My plan had always been to travel as extensively as my finances would allow and perhaps publish all my research on RAF Millom in a book; however my priority was my dad, whose health was steadily deteriorating. By this time, Phil and I were very much 'an item', and she decided that I should begin to meet her family. So we set out to stay with her brother Martin and his wife Pamela near Dumfries, Leaving on the Saturday morning to return home the following evening. The trip was made possible by my mother's sister, my Aunt Kathleen, who had been helping me over the months and had volunteered to check in on Dad during our short break.

On our return home the next day we were met at our door by a neighbour who told us that she had some bad news for us, we immediately thought it must be my Dad until she said, "I'm afraid that your auntie Kathleen died suddenly yesterday" we were lost for words and found my father stunned at the news, how ones life can change completely within 48 hours.

In September, Phil and I took a week's holiday on the Nile; my son John moved in with his grandfather in my absence which gave us total peace of mind, and the experience was fabulous, the Nile, the temples, the Valley of the Kings all met our expectations, and it was the first desired destination that I could cross off my very long list.

In October, having been admitted to Kendal hospital with respiratory complications, my Dad passed away peacefully; Phil and I visited him the day before, and he told us that the chaplain had spoken to him and given him a blessing, the chaplain told us later that he had said to my father "how are you Jack?", to which he replied "I'm in the departure lounge father!" he maintained his dry sense of humour to the very last.

CHAPTER SIXTEEN

Better days
Bruce Springsteen

In November 2006, Philippa, her son Russell and his wife Jane were flying out to India for a few weeks to stay in a little village in Goa called Arpora where her nephew Ian owned a villa, and I jumped at the chance to join them, Goa, home of the Vindaloo my favourite dish. The old cliché about going to India to 'find yourself' rang true; I didn't realise that I was missing until I went there. Ragging around barefoot in an old pair of shorts and tee-shirt, swimming in the Indian Ocean and fishing for catfish in the saltwater lagoons took me back to feeling like the carefree, irresponsible younger man I once was before I put a uniform on my back; it was to be the first of four visits to India for me, a country and a people I have become very fond of.

Philippa and I at a spice plantation

Myself and stepson-to-be, Russell at Anjuna Market

In July 2007, I got a phone call from my friends Bill and Maureen Teasdale in Perth, Australia, who told me that it was high time I visited them. On an impulse, I said I would be out next month, bought a ticket, and was with them by the first week in August. It was the start of two months of incredible adventures, and the Aussies are some of the most hospitable people on earth with that 'can do, no nonsense' attitude that we Brits seem to have lost as a nation. Covid has clipped my wings, but as soon as restrictions are lifted, I intend to return to Perth for some further late-night scrabble battles with the Teasdales. However, I have to say that based on past experience, I am no match for them; it seems that it's not just cricket, those Aussies are good at everything. I have now spent three long holidays in Australia and regret not taking the opportunity to emigrate when I was given a chance.

Digger bucket, Kalgoorlie super pit WA

Margaret river valley WA

Incredible wave rock, Hyden WA

Rottnest Island, off the coast of Fremantle WA

Postscript

When I left the prison service, my expressed intentions were to travel as extensively as possible and to try and write a book bringing together all my research into the history of RAF Millom. Until her retirement, I assisted Philippa in her house and animal sitting business, and over the years, our travels have been far and wide.

The book you are holding is the latest of six I have written, and so I can say that my years of retirement from the prison service have been happy and satisfying ones for me.

It was in 2010 that I received an unexpected plea for help from the RAF Millom museum team who informed me to my astonishment that in the years following my hand over to them, the museum had been made a limited company and had, it seemed, embarked upon a massive expansion of an ill-advised and wholly unsustainable nature. This resulted in a catastrophic liquidation that year for the scarcely believable sum of £250,000. All due to gross mismanagement and unpaid bills. I was devastated at the news but agreed to assist in returning loaned artefacts and photos to their rightful owners wherever possible; however, when I arrived at the museum to help do so, it was complete chaos with the premises resembling a cross between a scrapyard and a parish jumble sale and with the now elusive Mr Griffith nowhere to be seen.

Despite my best efforts, I could only stand by and watch the bulk of the museum's collection being auctioned off, a heartbreaking conclusion to so many years of goodwill and hard work.

On a much happier note, that is not the end of the RAF Millom story because, in 2012, I began work with the Millom Arts and Heritage Centre, which is based in the town railway station buildings, to gather what could be recovered from my original collection (much of which was then in private hands) and re-establishing a permanent exhibition on their premises. I am pleased to say that most of my photo archive was recovered along with a good number of exhibits, and by 2015 the RAF section occupied two rooms and encompassed the histories of RAF Millom, RAF Cark and RAF Walney, all three of the South Lakeland airfields.

Sat in Jetstream cockpit.

My partner Philippa and I were married in 2014 and have now been together some 18 years, all of them happy ones. She is an excellent travelling companion, and whilst our adventures have been many, the Coronavirus temporarily grounded us so we hope to resume our wanderings soon.

A Malta honeymoon. Seen here, two Spitfires at the Island's air museum

Our first anniversary dinner whilst working in Jersey, Channel Islands.

Some of our wanderings

It is impossible to fully encapsulate over three decades of prison service life in so few pages. I have done little more than give you some idea of its highs and lows whilst avoiding over moralising (though I have strong vows on many facets of the system) and avoiding it becoming the 'gore-fest' that prison books can be, good and positive things can be achieved in our prisons and most of the time it happens not because of funding but through rule-bending and innovation, the courage and conviction to 'think outside the box and to offer the opportunity for change no matter what the rule book says.

Would I join the prison service if I had my time to go over again?? No! You have not been paying attention; the whole bloody thing was an accident!

Lightning Source UK Ltd.
Milton Keynes UK
UKHW020650121122
412038UK00011B/295

9 781913 898397